CAN I HAVE YOUR ATTENTION?

INSPIRING BETTER WORK HABITS, FOCUSING YOUR TEAM, AND GETTING STUFF DONE IN THE CONSTANTLY CONNECTED WORKPLACE

CAN I HAVE YOUR ATTENTION?

CURT STEINHORST

with Jonathan McKee

WILEY

For general information about our other products and services, please contact our Customer Care Department within the United States at (800) 762-2974, outside the United States at (317) 572-3993, or fax (317) 572-4002.

Wiley publishes in a variety of print and electronic formats and by print-on-demand. Some material included with standard print versions of this book may not be included in e-books or in print-on-demand. If this book refers to media such as a CD or DVD that is not included in the version you purchased, you may download this material at http://booksupport.wiley.com. For more information about Wiley products, visit www.wiley.com.

Library of Congress Cataloging-in-Publication Data is Available:

ISBN 9781119390466 (Hardcover)
ISBN 9781119390480 (ePDF)
ISBN 9781119404385 (ePub)

Cover Design: Wiley

Printed in the United States of America

10 9 8 7 6 5 4 3 2 1

To Rand and Reed.

The moment you came into the world, you brought it all into focus.
You will always have my attention.

CONTENTS

FOREWORD

This may sound crazy, but I love chaos. I love noise. We all do. But noise is terrible for focus. Focus matters. The what, when, and why of focus shapes every part of our life. In a world where no one can focus on anything, being capable of it is an increasingly critical and unorthodox differentiator.

If you were to read my resume, the last thing you would think is "this guy is focused." I've always had an unorthodox approach to business and life in general. I have had a rap career (YouTube Jesse Jaymes for proof). I cofounded a private jet company that we sold to Warren Buffett. I partnered on a coconut water venture that was bought by Coca-Cola. Most recently, I hired a Navy SEAL to live with my family and wrote a book about the journey called *Living with a SEAL*.

Regardless of the optics, focusing on what's important is perhaps the single guiding tenant of every major life decision and stage. Life is too short to waste it on the unimportant. Yet the potential for distraction is always there for me. And I've fallen into that trap many times. I still do. That's why I recently went to live in a monastery. To get away from all the distractions. To shut off all the noise. However, living in a monastery isn't a realistic solution for most of us. That's what I love about the book you have in your hands.

Curt Steinhorst was introduced to me as someone who could help me focus my speech messages. He, in turn, helped me focus what I stand for. He is thoughtful. Not only as someone who has thrived in the distraction age—founding four successful start-up companies, speaking internationally on distraction and leadership—but as someone who has wrestled with the beast of distraction his entire life. Curt is not merely showing us how to cope. He knows distraction. Curt has not only had to overcome ADD, he has learned to overcome ADD in a time when the entire world has become immediately available, and he, in turn, immediately available to the world. Curt has not only learned to manage the demands of constant connection and technology, he has overcome them.

I like to encourage others: March to the beat of your own bongo drum. *Can I Have Your Attention?* is pioneering a new mindset. It's far too easy to let the noise of the world dictate the futures of our family, organization, community, and personal life. We can and must make intentional decisions about where we focus our attention, and put it toward the important things. That starts with you. I often remind others that they must cut the pie before sharing it. Take control of your time. You'll be surprised how much time you have to give to your family, your friends, your business when you eliminate the nonessentials. This book helps us get there.

Your business is a reflection of you. The better you are, the better your business will be. What's unique about *Can I Have Your Attention?* is that its concern is not so much distraction as it is the reason why we can't stay focused. Curt's goal isn't to create attention obsessed drones. With his eyes toward industry leaders and professionals, his goal is to help others become "Focus Wise"; to help leaders, professionals, spouses, and siblings reclaim their ability to focus.

In other words, no need to move in to the monastery full time. *Can I have Your Attention?* has the answers we need today.

Jesse Itzler
New York Times bestselling author
of "Living With a SEAL",
Co-Founder of Marquis Jet
and an owner of the Atlanta Hawks.

PROLOGUE:
YOU DON'T HAVE JACK

POPULAR HARRY

Everyone at work loves Harry, and it's easy to see why. He responds right away, at all hours (when does the guy sleep?) and in all places (including vacation, if necessary). "Team player" isn't strong enough to describe him. No one in his office makes phone calls anymore, but if they did, there's little doubt he would pick up.

Harry is the ideal of reachability in the digital age. Harry is a digital saint.

At 9 AM on Wednesday, Harry tackles a major case study due Friday. He's starting a day early, leaving nothing to chance.

By the third line, Harry stops midstroke. He needs Rachel's numbers from yesterday. After a quick Control S, he switches to e-mail and finds, among the 74 messages waiting there, an invite for a department meeting this afternoon. Is he even available?

Switching to his calendar, Harry sees "Vegas." He winces. The trip is only two weeks away, and he hasn't arranged travel yet. But Harry isn't just responsive; he's also responsible, which means he can't book a flight now . . . not without comparing prices (on a site that aggregates airlines and fares—only it's weird to him that they point to competing sites . . . or maybe they just *used* to be competitors? Convenience or a monopoly? This really nags at Harry).

Off the calendar and on to his browser to scan prices. He could swear one of the companies used a pitchman from the old *Star Trek* series. Harry's dad loved *Star Trek*, which reminds him that he needs to find the J. J. Abrams reboot on Netflix. Or is it on Amazon? He opens two new tabs to check—not on *either*? But there's nothing else to watch! His girlfriend hates when he says, "Get whatever," so he finds the trailer to a recent rom-com, which he then purchases on iTunes.

Thirty-five minutes later, Harry has booked a flight, watched three trailers, texted movie suggestions to his girlfriend, and added some shows he's heard about to their Netflix and Amazon lists. Now he can return to what he was doing.

What was he doing? Right, the case study.

Let's see, he was right about at . . . *the very beginning*.

Enigmatic Jack

I'd introduce you to Jack in person, but he's not available at the moment.

In fact, no one's been able to reach him for an hour or so. He's not answering e-mails, texts, or IMs. Some of his colleagues have even resorted to—brace yourself—looking up his work number and *dialing* it. Still nothing.

His colleagues have questions and issues they want addressed now. He needs to pay for his Girl Scout Cookies order. Why doesn't he ever come to the break room? The water cooler bottle is empty, and Cheryl keeps trying to hoist a new one into place. People want Jack's sign-off, his buy-in, his prompt *acknowledgment*.

So, where is Jack?

To be fair, Jack isn't taking an extended lunch or slipping out for a movie. You can find him in his office, or "vault," as he calls it. If you could look behind his closed door (guarded by a sign that says, "Let's catch up—later"), you wouldn't see him typing, tweeting, or texting. Instead, Jack leans back in his chair with his eyes open and fixed on nothing in particular, as though he's been thinking about something for a while.

If you want to break into Jack's vault, you have to do so in person. That might mean driving to his building, riding in an elevator, asking for directions to his office, then taking a deep breath as you prepare to knock (assuming the sign on his door doesn't dissuade you, which is clearly Jack's intention).

A colleague—or even worse, an employee—who reduces you to knocking?

Jack is an enigma in the digital age—reachable, but certainly not conveniently. Jack is a digital sinner.

And one more thing: Jack—everyone reluctantly agrees—is the most productive employee in the company.

SPOILER ALERT: HARRY WORKS FOR YOU

Maybe your "Harry" is a Stuart or a Lisa. Regardless of the name, the spirit of Harry and his distractions haunt your office. You have a Harry problem.

As his boss, you might be too busy to comprehend the saga of his wasted time and energy. Remember how Harry started early, "leaving nothing to chance"? In reality, he'd left everything to chance. It's why he stayed up nights scrambling against the deadline to finish his case study.

But when you read it, all is apparently right with the world. The work is delivered in typical Harry fashion. The numbers are accurate, the visuals helpful, the results actionable. Nice work from an employee whose talents have not disappointed you.

But they should disappoint you. Harry is robbing both you and himself.

What you don't know *does* hurt you—and your organization too. Nobody, including Harry, has a clue how far his potential could take him. What sort of case study could he have produced if he'd taken a page (actually, several) from Jack's book, eliminating distractions and sustaining a deep level of focus? On a larger scale, how much further along would he be professionally if this example wasn't a microcosm of his entire career?

But let's stop picking on Harry for a moment.

After all, he's just following the script of a typically distracted person in today's constantly connected workplace. His portrait is sketched from facts and supported by study after study.

U.S. adults spend 2.9 to 4.7 hours per day on smartphones alone.[1] Throw in TV, computers, and other forms of entertainment media and technology, and we clock in as many as 12 hours.[2] The average adult is awake only 15 hours a day. When are we exercising, meeting a friend for coffee, or playing with our children?

In homes nationwide, adults stare at a TV, teenagers stream video on smartphones, and toddlers flick colored shapes across tablets. If the dog is lucky, he has a treadmill because no one is walking him.

The overwhelming majority of us spend more time looking at screens than talking with our partners. And 88 percent of us actively engage with a second screen while watching TV.[3] We can't even remain focused on the device that used to be blamed for attention deficit disorder.

Why should you care what Harry does on his own time? Because his own time, and waste of it, bleeds into yours.

WHAT JACK'S REALLY DOING

Jack's phone is silent and out of sight, and though his laptop is open, he doesn't let it interrupt him. Put your ear to his door: You probably won't hear much. If you could peek inside, he might resemble the most useless and unproductive person in the building.

But Jack is far from that.

Since he closed his door an hour ago and politely but firmly asked the world to wait, Jack has been hatching an idea that could revolutionize how his company approaches the market. And since he learned to focus this way two years ago, he's been discovering pockets of potential and levels of ingenuity he never knew he had.

Every morning when Jack steps across the threshold of his vault, he becomes a different person. Even the sound of the latch clicking behind is a minor thrill. The devices he now stashes away without thought become, through his mastery of them, tools of focus instead of implements of distraction. The quote above his desk, from Spanish philosopher José Ortega y Gasset, is printed on yellowing paper but remains ever fresh.

"Tell me what you pay attention to, and I will tell you who you are."

Few words have done more to free up Jack's thinking. He likes to compare his job to spelunking into an uncharted cave, anticipating the depths he'll test and explore—in this case, the depths of his creativity and productivity.

Unlike the hunt for stalactites, this is no dedicated hobby. It's a work style made possible by a lifestyle that Jack embraces every day. Despite all his practice, it still takes a few minutes for Jack's senses to adjust to the sudden shift in worlds. But the relative silence and isolation don't unnerve him anymore.

By conventional workplace wisdom, these qualities compound Jack's sins. But to those who benefit from his work, he's a saint. Jack shines as a unique source of insight—that rare person who executes his ideas. And somehow he does this while leaving the office at a reasonable hour, unlike colleagues who spend more time at work but actually accomplish less.

Honestly, that guy. No one seems to know how he does it.

People like Jack swim against the current of mainstream thought—and may be the only real solution for organizations beset by increasing distraction and decreasing productivity. In this book, we'll build a case for why these employees are the most valuable assets of the digital age. And how you can help your own people become like him.

Jack isn't immune to the perils of the constantly connected workplace. What makes him exceptional is his capacity to block out noise and accomplish focused work. If you have one or more Jacks in your office, congratulations. More likely, you depend principally on Harry and his tribe. That's probably why you picked up this book in the first place.

WHAT THIS BOOK WILL DO FOR YOU

This book is for people who know they, their employees, and their organizations can be more productive but aren't sure how to get there. It's dedicated to harvesting our most precious, and dwindling, resource: attention. The digital age has no unique claim to the problem of focus. Everyone from Seneca to Shakespeare has wrestled with it. But they didn't have smartphones, Instagram, Facebook, e-mail, Netflix, or any of the other marvels (or scourges) that constantly challenge our focus today.

And I do mean "our" focus. I was diagnosed with attention deficit disorder (ADD) as a child. Distraction is the way my brain likes to work—whether I like it or not. The systems and strategies I recommend in this book started with a test subject of one.

As a father of two, I am woefully familiar with the difficult questions parents face related to connectivity and work-life balance. I am personally invested in the outcome of how we prepare the next generation for work and work for the next generation.

I run a business. I lead a team that wrestles with efficiency and empathy in the age of constant connectivity. We work with clients who expect immediate responses.

Perhaps the only difference: I've devoted my career, education, thought space, and financial resources to this challenge—so much so that I've coined a term to describe the goal of turning our attention resources into productivity. *Focus-wise* is what we should strive for, in work and in life. And I don't just believe this; I've made it a cornerstone of my business.

Focus wisdom is the difference between the strain of Harry and the satisfaction of Jack, between surrendering to distraction and mastering it. Between managing employees and inspiring them. Focus wisdom is a blueprint for organizational success.

WHERE WE'RE HEADED

This book is broken into seven sections, each section representing an aspect of the workplace that is affected by distraction. They can be read in sequence or mixed and matched to suit your needs:

- Section 1, *Nobody's Working*, outlines the nature of distraction in the constantly connected workplace, its hidden costs, and how we can start to address it.

- Section 2, *Finding Focus*, discusses the possibilities and limitations of our brain's ability to focus, including surprising truths about multitasking.

- Section 3, *Focus-Wise Space* makes a case for walls (literal and figurative) as a path to focus and explains the secret to Jack's success: the vault.

- Section 4, *Focus-Wise Technology*, describes our love–hate relationship with tech, how it can help promote focus, and the pros and cons of monitoring your people.

- Section 5, *Focus-Wise Communication*, unpacks the shortcomings of digital communication and how face-to-face communication can make all the difference.

- Section 6, *Focus-Wise Workday*, presents an alternative to the myth of work-life balance, explores useful delineation and delegation, and offers tips for extending focus and capacity.

- Section 7, *Focus-Wise Leadership* explores three questions to determine proper focus, the secret of a focus culture, training that works, the power of emotional engagement, and the surprising cure for employee boredom.

HOW TO READ THIS BOOK

Although shorter is better for a book like this, useful things can be left out. That's why I've provided a host of helpful resources for you at focuswise.com/book. Here you can consult a constantly updated repository of expanded content and practical advice.

If you're like me, you may want some personal and professional high-level *reflection* as you dive in. Journaling has been a tremendous way for me to begin and end each of my days in a focused way. There are reflection questions for every chapter at focuswise.com/book.

Plus, I have created a deep-dive video for each of the seven sections, providing a strategic way to frame *discussion* with your team about that section's content. Let's be honest—few people read more than 140 characters these days. Perhaps gathering to watch the video together will help start needed conversations within your team.

From there, I hope they pick up/download a copy of this book themselves! In fact, check out the intro video as soon as you finish reading the prologue.

Finally, I know many of us are ready for practical solutions to this well-known (and personally played out) problem of distraction. You want ground-level resources to begin *implementation* of focus-wise solutions within your team or organization. Thus, you will also find pertinent and actionable resources specific to each section at www .focuswise.com/book.

What we are asking you to do in this book isn't easy: to rethink virtually every aspect of work today. From how you lead, hire, and train to how you run your meetings and even set up your office space. We are asking you to do the hard work so your people have a fighting chance to reclaim their focus and thrive in the constantly connected workplace.

The good news is it's more possible—and way more valuable— than you might think.

The power of true focus awaits you and your people. Together, we'll learn how to cultivate and maintain it.

SECTION ONE

NOBODY'S WORKING

CHAPTER 1

The Curse of the Overwhelmed

Twenty-two.

That's how many e-mails have arrived in the past 15 minutes as I've tried to write this opening. And because I indulged the temptation to check, I'll work longer and get less done today. I probably won't even realize it.

Been here before? Know someone who has?

You're not alone. Ask your people how work is going and you'll hear:

I'm burning it at both ends.

So much on my plate, it's crazy.

Putting in 14-hour days.

Sure, people feel overworked, but that's not the problem. We confuse busyness and activity with actual work, so what feels like *overworked* is actually *overwhelmed*. What's the difference? To find out, let's go back to my inbox.

Of those 22 e-mails, three were from employees, one was from a client, one was from a prospect, and five were newsletters or promotions.

The other 12? They were from people who were supposed to be working. *But weren't.*

These are friends who work in fields like consulting, accounting, medicine, journalism, and software sales, sending messages such as, "Where did you buy that Ninja blender?" at 10:30 AM on a Tuesday. Twelve out of 22 isn't bad—one study says 86 percent of the e-mails we get aren't critical for work.[1]

HEY, I'M DOING MY JOB

Most people don't think distractions affect their productivity. They are distracted, they say, but they still get to what needs to be done. As someone who has studied distraction for years, I can tell you that very few people are honest about its cost in their lives, and almost none have realistic strategies to overcome it. They think they're working harder and more efficiently than ever. *But they've never actually worked less.*

Since 2007 (the same year, notably, that the iPhone was released), the decline in employee productivity has been staggering. One efficiency expert says we can lose more than six hours a day to interruptions.[2] Another estimates that these interruptions waste 28 billion hours a year, costing the U.S. economy nearly $1 trillion.[3] A different study about multitasking—a mantra for many employers—found that it costs the economy $450 billion annually.[4]

While productivity has plummeted, connectivity—the extent to which we have access to one another—hasn't.

And with all that constant connection, the borders between work and life are crumbling.

In one survey, 87 percent of employees admitted to reading political social media posts at work.[5] Other research shows that 60 percent of all online purchases occur between 9 AM and 5 PM and that 70 percent of U.S. porn viewing also happens during working hours[6] ("working" from home?). And if none of that convinces you, perhaps this will: Facebook's busiest hours are 1 to 3 PM—right in the middle of the workday.

So maybe it's not surprising when the latest Gallup poll finds that the majority of employees worldwide aren't engaged in their work.[7]

And yet all these studies might only scratch the surface, relying as they do on the perceptions of people who want to think they're working. How much time do *you* actually spend on uninterrupted work? How much time do your people?

Yet it's hard to imagine returning to a time when employees like Harry were less accessible and lacked powerful tools at their fingertips 24/7. In truth, we love being able to reach the Harrys in our lives anytime, anywhere. You can call or e-mail him. You can chat via IM because he's usually active. You can text, tweet, or even tap him on the shoulder, since he's probably nearby. No matter your method, he'll respond right away—which is why so many of his colleagues consider him a saint.

But whether those who depend on him know it or not, Harry is far from sainthood when it comes to productivity. Harry commits sins of omission. He fails to accomplish even half of what he's capable of. Although he may get high marks, his actual value has never been lower.

It's easy to blame the employees. But I've got some hard news: The problem is with you.

CHAPTER 2

It's Not Their Fault

Today's employees aren't lazy, entitled, belligerent, unethical, or incompetent. (Although there are always exceptions.) Many of them simply haven't known a world in which they weren't chronically busy and connected—and the rest are forgetting what this seemingly mythical world looked like.

Historically, employees have never had so much within immediate reach . . . while being so immediately reachable.

They've never processed so much information . . . while retaining so little.

They've never been more connected . . . while facing so many interruptions.

They've never been so distracted.

Distracted (dis'traktəd), adjective: unable to concentrate because one's attention is diverted by something that amuses or entertains.

Our devices and the constant connection they bring keep us in a perpetual state of distraction. The amusing consequences of distraction have become distractions themselves: a viral video of a woman at an NBA game smacked in the face by a basketball, another of a woman falling into a mall fountain, still another of a man strolling straight up to a bear. (Bonus points if you make it through this chapter without looking them up.)

And then there are the seriously tragic stories: a woman hit by a bus, a hiker walking off a cliff, a driver veering into a semi—all while staring at a phone, oblivious to the world around them.

Sometimes the device is a pair of headphones and the casualty someone's career. A chief financial officer of a publicly traded investment firm once asked me to coach an employee he was on the verge of firing because his ears were always covered. The CFO liked his work. The employee was a top producer in the company. He was still one step away from getting fired.

Our attention has never been more coveted and correspondingly depleted. We're so used to being entertained by cat massage videos (please tell me you've seen them) that we struggle with *sustained* thinking—the very kind of thinking that is required to innovate in business. In the workplace, leaders tend to favor either the "one-man band" multitasker who lacks focus or the employee who is so hyper-focused that she ignores other priorities. What's needed is a realistic model of focused attention.

MORE VALUABLE THAN CASH

"Pay attention!" was my teachers' favorite thing to say to me. Turns out the phrase dates to the fourteenth century, affirming attention's long standing as a form of payment (I still owe my teachers substantial back payments). In the constantly connected workplace, the command has become much more than a metaphor. "Attention is the real currency of businesses and individuals," Tom Davenport writes in *The Attention Economy*, adding that it can be traded, purchased, and "converted into other currencies."[1]

Herbert Simon framed this currency for the Information Age: "What information consumes is rather obvious: It consumes the attention of its recipients. Hence a wealth of information creates a poverty of attention."

If attention is currency, the job of a leader is to help employees get rich. Companies pay big bucks to learn what we want to see and how to get us to opt in. For your people, the stakes are even higher: Attention buys both material *and* intrinsic satisfaction. Your success as a leader will be measured by how well they spend their hard-earned share.

In the constantly connected workplace, attention is squandered on hundreds of insignificant requests, offers, and alluring inquires. The Digital Age delivers the world to us, but it also delivers *us* to the world. Smartphones, e-mail, live-stream videos, and social apps put us in higher demand than ever before. Place and time, "at home" and "after hours," no longer exist. No matter where your people are, the people in their lives are constantly demanding their attention.

Naturally, they feel worn down—even paralyzed—by infinite demands. It's amazing they get anything done at all. Odysseus could steer past the deadly but seductive Sirens, but would he have stood a chance against e-mail, Facebook, and the latest Snapchat filter?

The plight of the constantly connected isn't about weakness or willpower. Those e-mail, text, and "like" notifications can elevate the production of oxytocin and dopamine in the same way a drug addiction does.[2]

Oxytocin and dopamine are powerful neurochemicals. Dopamine—the "pleasure" chemical—is tied to experiences like eating, sex, and drugs. "Our brains are wired to ensure that we will repeat life-sustaining activities by associating those activities with pleasure or reward," according to the National Institute on Drug Abuse.[3] When drugs—or social media—feel "life-sustaining," our brains are just doing their job all too well. Poor focus is the natural consequence of this neurochemical rush. Distracted employees are present without really being there, like the hapless people-slash-fuel source in *The Matrix*.

In the movie (spoiler alert), human beings lose themselves in a virtual world of endless seductions divorced from the messy, difficult reality known as Zion. (Sound like the Internet?) The problem, of course, is that it's not real. They're actually resting in a coma-induced cocoon while their bodies are being used as batteries to feed the machine. But the machines learned that give humans a virtual experience and neurochemical euphoria (i.e., girl in restaurant), and they will contentedly remain in a helpless and dependent stupor. However, while most of the world lives in bliss inside this fake world, a few know the truth, have unplugged, and are fighting for the rest. All goes haywire when Cypher, a long-time member of Morpheus' (Laurence Fishburne) rebel team decides—over a steak dinner and a presumably expensive glass of Cabernet with Agent Smith—that it's worth betraying his team in exchange for the hollow but alluring life in the Matrix. His one major condition: that he remember nothing of the real world. For him, ignorance was bliss. Better to escape into a sea of distraction than be forced to engage life on real terms. He chose distraction at a life-threatening cost to his team. More disturbing than the film itself is how prophetic the story has become. And in the real world, employees (and leaders) addicted to connectivity aren't just selling out their organizations and teams; they are also selling out themselves.

Distraction wins.

Focus loses.

Productivity plummets.

Efficiency becomes a myth.

And companies are starting to take notice.

How do I know? Because I'm the guy they hire to fix the problem.

CHAPTER 3

Tools of Our Tools

Throughout my childhood, I struggled to keep focused. When I was 12 years old, a doctor diagnosed me with attention deficit disorder. The challenge took a new shape as I left the confines of academia to enter the workforce in my early 20s. Bursts of extreme focus and a knack for digesting concepts couldn't make up for the dozens of small tasks required to succeed in my first j-o-b. Ever since, I have been fascinated with what causes someone to pay attention or not. Why were there times when focusing seemed as natural to me as breathing and others when I couldn't keep from being distracted if my life depended on it? I wanted to learn: What is attention? How does it work? How can we harness the power of it?

I pored through thousands of hours' worth of the latest research and interviewed leaders in neuroscience, social science, psychology, philosophy, and tech. Using myself—and eventually my company—as the lab rat, I experimented with ways to reduce distraction and improve focus. I spoke with CEOs and managers around the world—all of whom struggled to get their employees (and for many, themselves) to focus on the right things at the right time.

I saw that distraction affected every level of our professional culture. Questions like these haunted everyone, from small business owners to Fortune 100 executives:

What can we do about our e-mail problem?

How do we promote focus in an office of constant connectivity?

How do I get my people to stop wasting the whole day on their damn phone?

How do I avoid blowing a gasket the next time I see a millennial on Instagram at work?

Over the past six years, I've given speeches to hundreds of companies, consulted with some of the nation's most successful companies, and jumped into the trenches with CEOs and managers around the world—all with the goal of helping employees, leaders, and whole organizations deal with distraction. These organizations know all too well the challenges of overload, distraction, and constant connectivity. They don't know what to do about it. How can you preserve the benefits of accessibility without bringing with it all the chronic interruptions? Can you create an environment where attention is cherished and focus reigns?

Many leaders misdiagnose the problem altogether. Maybe you're one of them.

TECHNOLOGY IS NOT THE PROBLEM

A client from a major financial institution recently asked me, "Can you help us reduce the number of e-mails we get every day?"

There's a surprisingly simple answer to this issue: It's called batch processing—waiting to review all of your e-mails together a few times a day, rather than continuously. I could have flown out to his office, spent 15 minutes teaching the technique, two hours eating a steak dinner with a $100 bottle of wine (both expensed), and then sent him the bill. Problem solved.

But inbox overload was just a symptom, not the disease. The client never thought to ask: Why is there so much e-mail in the first place?

MILLENNIALS ARE NOT THE PROBLEM

As a certified speaker for the Center for Generational Kinetics, the number one millennial and generation Z research firm in the United States, I have addressed more than 200 audiences on the topic of how to bridge the generational divide. There's no complaint I haven't heard. The most prevalent: Millennials won't get off their phones.

I sympathize—with the phone part. The problem of distraction and constant connectivity affects *employees of all ages*, not just one demographic. According to a Nielsen report,[1] for example, generation X spends 6 hours and 58 minutes a week on social media—10 percent more than millennials. And gen Xers' time on everything from Twitter to Pinterest is increasing at a faster rate as well. Baby boomers are jumping on even more rapidly, which—perhaps—contributes to why gen Z is jumping off.[2]

Just as telling: Millennials consume far less media overall than their older counterparts, clocking in at 26 hours and 49 minutes per week. Gen X? Thirty-one hours and 40 minutes.[3]

POOR PRODUCTIVITY IS NOT THE PROBLEM

But the overall problem isn't just about productivity. Constant connectivity affects every part of our personal, professional, and organizational lives. Recognize these symptoms?

- Your meetings lack focus and meaningful action. Some folks engage, but most duck into their phones or laptops—and everyone knows Chris is messaging the new intern.

- You and your employees have never been more in contact and less in sync. Missing is a deep sense of community, especially face-to-face communication.

- You and those you lead struggle to handle conflict and difficult conversations, especially in person. Empathy and "people skills" (once fodder for jokes about job candidates who lack "real" skills) have waned.

- Your organizational boundaries are fuzzy. Forget dedicated collaborative spaces—every room has essentially become the same room in terms of activity, behavior, and expectations.

- The boundary between work and home is even worse. Working from home can be a plus—so why are both productivity and domestic life suffering?

- Your well-prepared message fails to resonate amid shrinking attention spans. True audience engagement is elusive.

  Clearly we're facing multiple battlefronts. But unwavering focus on one skirmish means getting outflanked from other directions. The key is to reassess every aspect of work.

THE PROBLEM IS MUCH DEEPER—AND MUCH MORE COSTLY

The truth is, we'll never be moved to act until we clearly understand the cost of constant connectivity. (Most of us don't even know we're in the red.)

  It costs your people time. A study from the University of Michigan revealed that multitasking results in a 40 percent drop in efficiency.[4] That's more than three hours each workday. All the while, your people stress over not having enough time for their responsibilities.

  It costs them quality. In a fascinating study, Dr. Harold Pashler of the University of California at San Diego tested the production of Harvard MBAs. When he added a second, basic task to their workload, their performances dropped to the level of an 8-year-old.[5] Of course, the natural conclusion to all this is either help sharpen your employees' focus or save money by hiring second-graders.

  It robs them of creativity. In the face of information overload, we fail to store new ideas in long-term memory. That means forgetting anniversaries and, more seriously, jeopardizing our creative thinking (though, come to think of it, I'm not sure anything is more serious than forgetting your anniversary). The magic happens when we connect ideas already in our brains that were never connected before. The more we can pull from memory, the more connections our brains can make. *Voilà*—creativity. Without the space to process or connect, your people can become virtual mockingbirds. They figuratively (and sometimes literally) retweet the hottest new ideas, but none of it gets stored on their mental hard drives. This means less material for later connections, which means less creative and critical thinking.

  It erases meaning and purpose. Employees need time to consider the significance of their work. Engagement springs from the gaps that help us understand the "why" behind our endeavors. But there simply isn't space for purposeful reflection when your people jump from e-mail to meetings to texts to tweets to podcasts to sports updates—and finally to the pillow.

The ultimate cost is unhappy, burned-out employees who further retreat to their devices for escape or connection with people who also feel stuck at work.

THE PROBLEM

In the words of Henry David Thoreau, "Men have become the tools of their tools." We have lost control of our ability to choose where we spend our attention and instead become slaves of distraction. But there is a way out. Over the rest of this book, I break down the complex and systemic problem of distraction step by step and apply tangible, proven solutions that can be used in any workplace. To get on top of it, you have to rethink the following areas.

Communication

Consider the number of ways you can be reached, how you communicate with your people, and the interruptions that result. Is e-mail the one place for everything? Can we reduce inbox clutter? Does texting and messaging interfere or help? Would shorter meetings be more effective? Should we put phones and laptops aside, or keep them at the ready? Can conflict ever be handled digitally, or should it always be face to face?

Technology

Are you providing helpful technology or needless distractions for your people? Can they access key information, or does it get lost in the shuffle? (A friend at a major consulting firm once told me they estimated that 95 percent of operations and research writing goes unread by everyone but those who produced it.) Do you use productivity software? A Web search of "to do list apps" brings 1.3 billion results. Are any of them helpful, or does the learning curve sap the very resources they're meant to preserve?

Office Design and Work Location

Is your workplace conducive to work...or distractions? What about telecommuters? Can we create synergy on a team that's physically separated?

Planning

Do your people know why they're there, and can they articulate it? Is your company good at prioritizing? Do managers know the difference between delegation and empowerment? Do they hold on to too much or too little?

People Development

How are people promoted in your workplace? Promotions are often tied to social connectivity, perhaps the last thing you want in a hire. Is work-life balance a cliché or a priority? Do spouses expect to reach us at work and do bosses expect to reach us at home? How do you tailor training to dwindling attention spans? Or should you?

Leadership

Are you a leader who develops new leaders? How do you motivate when studies show 87 percent of employees aren't engaged?[6] Can a paycheck make them care? How does authority change when everyone has equal access to endless information? And what about yourself needs to change before you can lead the needed change in your organization?

ARE YOU PART OF THE SOLUTION?

Be warned: More challenging questions are coming, and some of the answers might shock you. (Should you let your people watch more cat videos? Research says yes!)

And for leaders, the responsibility is immense. It's your job to provide the tools, training, and incentives to help employees focus on the right thing at the right time. Organizations sabotage themselves by rewarding attention-killers: ill-timed meetings, 24/7 availability, immediate responses, and the endless sharing of information. If you've set that pace, it's time to unset it.

In other words, it's time to be part of the solution. And it starts with finding focus.

NOW THAT I HAVE YOUR ATTENTION...

For Section 1 reflection questions, summary video, and next step resources, please visit focuswise.com/cihya/one

SECTION TWO

FINDING FOCUS

CHAPTER 4

The Science of Attention

To be focus-wise is to effectively allocate our attention at a particular moment in a particular context. It's an art that emerges through careful practice, a right understanding of how our brains work, and sensitivity to the professional and personal worlds around us.

As a kid, I could spend hours playing video games. Hours. My mom would call for dinner and I wouldn't even hear her. I was completely enraptured. Then Monday came. I couldn't finish a single page of the fill-in-the-blank homework assignment. What leads one brain to spend hours uncovering the complex mysteries of the world and another to spend hours scrolling their feed or binge-watching an entire series on Netflix?

OUR TWO SYSTEMS OF ATTENTION

Our brains are hardwired to pay attention in two very contradictory ways, each serving a distinct purpose in keeping us alive.[1] The first works by responding to new stimuli in order to seek pleasure or avoid pain. The second enables us to make active decisions about where we will focus in order to accomplish a goal.

System 1: Bottom-Up Attention

Humanity has survived in large part because chemicals in our brains attract us to new stimuli. When seeing something novel, we receive— you guessed it—a jolt of dopamine. Neuroscientists call this *bottom-up attention*, and it's the first system of attention in our brains. Bottom-up attention seeks new and novel stimuli with a particular focus on finding pleasure (i.e., procreation) and avoiding pain (i.e., death). If you are in a jungle, the earlier you see a lion running at you, the better your odds of your buddy being food and not you. Your immediate needs are driven by system 1.

System 1 is great for survival, but it makes it very hard to focus. You can think of system 1 as a pile of kids in the backseat of a minivan on a road trip. Their sole mission is to avoid boredom, so they look out the window for fascinating cars or funny-looking animals, they play with toys and video game devices, and they poke and bother each other—all in the name of finding entertainment. As we go through life, this system of attention is always looking out for things that will excite us and that we want to go toward while also watching out for things that cause us pain, which we naturally flee.

System 2: Top-Down Attention

Lucky for us, there is another part of our brain that is devoted to planning. System 2, the executive control or *top-down system*, allows us to make active decisions about where we will focus. Our brain's second system of attention is centered on tasks or the desire to accomplish goals. You can think of system 2 as the parent in the driver's seat of that minivan, trying to get the kids safely and soundly to the destination. Unlike the kids, who only see stimuli as opportunities for pleasure or pain, the system 2 parent sees new stimuli in the context of her overall goal—will it help her reach that goal or keep her from it?—and she works hard to push away threats in order to keep focus. System 2 is what enables us to choose to wash our car, clean our rooms, and file our taxes (or at least an extension). Your future self loves it when this system of your attention wins.

The secret to effectively allocating our attention is knowing when and how to engage your top-down system and when to just let the bottom-up system do its thing.

BROKEN MODELS

In my consulting work, I regularly encounter two misguided ideals about focus. One holds that an employee should juggle multiple tasks, respond immediately, and complete work with no regard for volume, variety, and changing priorities. The other rejects multi-tasking outright, insisting that an employee hyperfocus on one task to block out distractions. Why would they ever take their eyes off a spreadsheet? They have a single job. They should just do it.

The first employee can't focus. The second risks becoming a robot (and eventually being replaced by one). And neither one accurately understands the human relationship with multitasking.

The One-Man Band

Every workplace has self-proclaimed multitaskers. They type with one hand and scroll through their Facebook timeline with the other, all while talking into a headset on a conference call. They look impressively busy—even efficient. After all, they're halfway through 17 different tasks.

If only they could finish just one of them well.

These employees commonly don't recognize their lack of productivity and effectiveness. They think they're a one-man band.

Dick Van Dyke, as Bert the chimney sweep, literally *is* a one-man band at the beginning of *Mary Poppins*. Bert wows us by strapping on every conceivable instrument, from drums to bass, playing them all simultaneously before using his forehead to smash the cymbal at the finale. He may have lost brain cells, but onlookers break out in thunderous applause.

In a similar way, today's organizations applaud people who jump from task to task, always available, willing to drop whatever they're doing at a whim. We reward their ability to multitask. We even put it in job descriptions (these were taken from actual job postings):

- "Multitasking Office Rockstars Needed. We are looking for talented people to work in a relaxed office atmosphere." Relaxed?

- "Multitasking Security Officer." Hope the person they hired isn't writing reports while subduing a shoplifter.

- "Multitasking Administrative Assistant/Receptionist...who can handle multiple tasks at once, successfully. Attention to detail is a MUST." Attention to detail? The ad shows a weirdly grinning man doing the job—with six arms.

As a leader, you might realize that this type of multitasking from your employees is bad for business. What you may not consider is that if you expect an immediate response from your staff, you are demanding it from them.

The Focus Savant

Novak Djokovic epitomizes today's hyperfocused athlete. ESPN once detailed the tennis phenom's brutal regimen.[2] He began each morning hitting balls, then stretching, drinking recovery fluids, visiting his trainer, getting a massage, strategizing with his coach, and doing yoga. All part of a day that included three 90-minute practices in front of an army of specialists who poked, prodded, and assessed the star.

Every aspect of Djokovic's life was monitored: diet, sleep, TV, even video games. He began emotional counseling, color therapy, meditation, and visualization.

And you know what? Djokovic became number one in the world, winning 43 straight matches and multiple titles from 2010 to 2011, including Wimbledon and the U.S. Open.

Many of my clients are pro athletes who covet the same kind of focus. They don't seem to have a choice. Their competition has never trained harder, eaten smarter, hired better coaches, or used more expensive equipment.

Imagine an employee who devotes that kind of focus to, say, expense reports. Charlene's one job is to study receipts: what's allowed, what's not, and whether her colleagues have used approved hotels and airlines. She can scan a receipt with 48 items and pick out the one illegitimate expense in milliseconds.

Charlene is also burned out—and this close to quitting.

What if an employee couldn't be reached *at all* during a three-week project?

"Where's Jason?"

"He's working on the Anderson account. He can't be disturbed—*until July*."

Leaders who reject multitasking as wasteful slingshot to the myth of the focus savant. Eliminate all distractions, they reason, and productivity soars. This is not only dangerous during a fire drill, but it also ignores both our biological wiring and how most workplaces operate today.

Afterall, Charlene isn't Novak Djokovic, and it's unrealistic to expect her to be.

THE MAGICAL MYSTERIES OF MULTITASKING

Unless you've been under a rock, you've probably come across at least one of a plethora of articles claiming that we can't multitask. The dynamics of and science behind multitasking, it turns out, are a lot more complex than you might think.

One Sphere (or Why You Can't Multitask)

Our brains can devote active focus to *only one sphere of attention* at a time.[3] When people say humans can't multitask, this is what they are referring to. When we try to manage two active focus tasks at once, the results are pretty pathetic.

Two cognitive neuroscientists[4] set up a driving simulator, and one said to the other, "I call frontal lobe!" (Get it? Front-al lobe?) No, but seriously: They had 200 participants navigate highway traffic while responding to cellphone questions about math and object categorization and then recall the items in a certain order. Each was a simple task when done separately. Three percent passed the test—a failure rate of *97 percent*. Then there's the British experiment in which people who tried to juggle work with e-mails and texts lost 10 IQ points.[5] That's the equivalent of missing a whole night's sleep and more than double the effect of smoking marijuana. Ergo, the question "What, were you high when you made this decision?" should be changed to "What, were you multitasking when you made this decision?" When it comes to true focus, we are single-sphered creatures.

We can't even switch between active focus tasks well. A group of doctors conducted four experiments in which young people shifted between activities like solving math problems and categorizing geometric objects.[6] Every participant in the study lost time when switching tasks. The more complex the task, the more time they lost through switching.

Task switching isn't impossible. It just takes time to refocus whenever we're yanked into a different sphere of attention. And not all types of refocusing are the same. Glancing at a calendar pop-up or text—even quickly answering it—hinders us less than fully diving into a completely new sphere, for instance. However, the research consistently shows that whenever we switch our attention from one task and refocus it onto another, we lose productivity. Multitaskers convinced of their own efficiency should add up the time lost switching from project to project. (Of course, that would be another task switch.)

So why do we compulsively switch tasks, even when it hurts our productivity? The problem is with our old friend dopamine: Switching to a new task triggers a shot of dopamine in our brain because our brains reward what's new. Instead of experiencing the costs of refocusing, multitaskers experience the rewards of entertaining something new. Which, in turn, makes them *feel* productive.

It boils down to this: When we switch spheres of attention, our overall efficiency drops dramatically. No one-man band can justify that many wrong notes.

Mastery (or Why You Can Multitask)

But here's where things get interesting: Within a single sphere, the number of activities we can manage at once depends on our mastery and experience with that sphere. A professional drummer is a phenomenal multitasker—he has mastered his given sphere enough to free himself for other tasks within that sphere. He taps the bass with his left foot, the cymbal with his right, and myriad other drums using his hands, all at the same time. (I, on the other hand, lose rhythm by adding a toe-tap while clapping my hands.) The drummer can't do his taxes while making music, but within the sphere of attention he's mastered, he can do a lot. Recent research reveals that our brains are capable of handling a remarkable amount of tasks—if we get the timing and the types of tasks right. Marketing professor Steven Sweldens and two colleagues conducted exhaustive research that supports something each of us already knows: When we're "in the zone," we can overcome distraction, extend our focus far beyond our norm, and accomplish almost anything.[7]

Autopilot: Multitasking That Increases Productivity. Our professional drummer can probably do something that's outside his sphere of attention—as long as it's something simple. You and I do this kind of multitasking all the time. It's like when you perform a routine of chores while talking on the phone. You can focus fully on Uncle George's latest healthy eating advice because you're drying and stacking dishes on autopilot (and maybe on mute as well). In fact, combining one easy task (like listening to classical music) and one hard task (like financial modeling), can actually increase your overproductivity.

Inhibitory Spillover: Multitasking That Increases Our Willpower. In a fascinating study, Sweldens' colleague Mirjam Tuk found that people fighting the urge to go to the bathroom made smarter impulse-control choices (i.e., focused on a spreadsheet rather than flipping to WhatsApp).[8] She hypothesized that bladder control fires up the brain's inhibitory network, which is tied to cognitive control[9] (the part of your brain you use when you are actively deciding what to focus on). This is called inhibitory spillover—meaning when you resist one thing, it actually *increases* resistance across the board. It works like a vaccine. You give yourself a small amount of the virus, and your body is now equipped to fight a full outbreak.

Sweldens et al. followed up with a study in which subjects with a bowl of Pringles in front of them watched a muted video of a woman speaking. Some participants were asked to avoid looking at the subtitles. "Viewers who had been given the instruction ate fewer chips than those who watched freely," Sweldens reported.[10] This means that when you mentally work to avoid something, you are more likely to avoid doing something else you shouldn't do—like eat delicious Pringles. (Yes, I'm a Pringles guy.)

So, what does this mean for you? On the one hand, if you switch spheres, you sacrifice both time and quality. On the other hand, some forms of multitasking actually improve focus. It's all about what tasks are involved.

FULL FOCUS, MEDIUM FOCUS, LIGHT FOCUS

Tasks essentially come in three focus sizes: full, medium, and light (Figure 4.1).

Full-Focus Tasks

Full-focus tasks can be done effectively only one at a time. These are activities like actively listening to a coworker present important financial information, writing that all-team e-mail about staffing changes, reading a book with an aim to actually remember it, or spending some quality time critically thinking through a problem you are trying to solve. Trying to do more than one full-focus activity at a time comes with a cost. This is what most people who refer to multitasking in a negative way mean.

Medium-Focus Tasks

Medium-focus tasks sit between full and light. This might be answering simple e-mail questions, scrolling through your Twitter feed, doing your laundry, or vegging out in front of the TV.

You can pair medium-focus tasks together as long as you recognize that, though you may be doing two things at the same time, you are not actually simultaneously processing any information. You are also switching between spheres, which means there are productivity consequences.

When you pair medium tasks together, quality and speed suffers. But that's not necessarily a bad thing, especially when the alternative to slow is not at all. When I'm on the road, I will reply to a ton of e-mails while having sports or a mediocre comedy in the background. I recognize I'm not actually watching most of whatever is on TV, but the occasional joke or highlight score entertains me, fulfilling

Full Focus

Activities that benefit from moving information into long-term memory storage, involve problem solving, precise timing, and critical thinking.

Medium Focus

Activities for which long-term memory storage is not important.

Light Focus

Activities that demand few resources; these can serve to enhance focus on other more demanding activities.

Hint: try attaching light activities to heavier tasks. They might help!

Figure 4.1   Task-Pairing Chart.

my brain's craving for new and novel stimuli while I'm knocking out work I would otherwise avoid. In other words, switching between medium-focus tasks is for moments when the debate is between doing no work or doing moderately easy work that I don't want to waste my peak focus moments on.

Basically, I use one medium task to intentionally distract myself from another medium task that my brain tells me is painful. The audiobook I am actively concentrating on makes cleaning the dishes less miserable.

Conversely, some medium-focus tasks are categorically dangerous when paired together. For instance, if one of the spheres requires your vision to effectively operate a motorized vehicle, flipping to another sphere that requires you to read a text is a very bad idea. When pairing mental and physical tasks, the physical task moves from active focus to a region of the brain where autopilot runs. Autopilot is good when the task is predictable and easy. It is not good at dealing with the rare outlier (like a couch on the highway).

Task pairing decreases your likelihood of remembering anything. When you increase the inputs, you increase your cognitive load, which makes it tough for information to move from your short-term to your long-term memory.

Pairing also disconnects you emotionally from both tasks. Emotional engagement requires your consistent attention on a subject. If you are scrolling through Twitter while watching *Game of Thrones*, you are far less likely to care when (spoiler alert) Ned Stark dies tragically. You may have already discovered this and used it to your advantage—chatting with your friend during a scary scene in a movie, for instance.

Light-Focus Tasks

Light tasks, such as doodling or listening to certain kinds of music, can actually enhance focus by canceling out distractions and subtly stimulating the brain. A study led by Ravi Mehta from the University of Illinois Urbana-Champaign revealed that moderate ambient noise (like that at a coffee shop) improved creativity noticeably.[11] Sweldens et al. recommend such activities for staying in the zone.

However, different people react differently to light-focus tasks. They can be helpful or harmful depending on your brain chemistry and the tasks involved.

And no, listening to the top 40 isn't a focus enhancer. Stop it. Neither is having social media on your second screen. If the task requires you to hear and process words, it's not a light-focus activity.

Movement, especially in the form of exercise, however, seems to help. A University of Florida study found that people with Parkinson's disease improved their cognitive performance while riding exercise bikes.[12] Researchers hypothesized that "cognitive arousal" occurs when people gird themselves for a challenging cognitive task. Also, exercise activates parts of the brain that control movement. This arousal spurs the release of neurotransmitters that boost brain speed and efficiency, making motor and cognitive activities more successful. Many successful CEOs tout walking meetings, a great pairing of a light-focus and a full-focus task.

Multitasking isn't all or nothing. It's a matter of knowing what works (mastering a skill that frees you for other tasks) and what doesn't (switching between spheres of attention). Yes, you can answer a quick IM and get back to that report. No, you can't respond to 10 important e-mails and still contribute to the meeting. It's about, as stated from the outset, effectively allocating our attention.

CHAPTER 5

Focus-Wise in the Age of Distraction

Your people will zone out during meetings, text their spouses, and check Facebook at their desks. Human beings will always be distracted. The secret is learning how to engineer distraction to your organization's benefit.

That doesn't mean hiring "expert" multitaskers or demanding focus savants. It means encouraging and equipping employees to be focus-wise.

And we have to be realistic about what's possible in the constantly connected workplace. Over and over, I hear leaders equate distraction with theft: "If you check social media during work, you're stealing." Do they apply the same logic the other way around?

Life intrudes on work just as work intrudes on life (often to the advantage of an organization).

As leaders, we need to recognize the glut of commitments and obligations each employee faces at work and outside of it. Your project manager has a crucial meeting at 4 PM—someone will have to pick up her son from soccer practice. Three e-mails are marked "urgent," but which one really is? Did she remember to DVR the season finale of her favorite show?

A well-balanced person learns to wear many hats. But eventually one of those hats will demand to be worn when another ball cap is already in place. In other words, the more responsibilities, the more chance of *bleed-through*.

Bleed-through isn't necessarily bad. For example, if your people can text you at home with a quick question, they gain the freedom to keep working and you can avoid staying late at the office. This creates overall efficiency.

But bleed-through can work the other way as well. Your spouse may feel justified in texting you all day at work. Endless exchanges, of course, breed *inefficiency*. Two ball caps worn in opposite directions might make you look like Sherlock Holmes, but they won't give you his powers of deduction. Distraction isn't a test of employee loyalty or willpower—if it was, we'd all fail.

Today's constantly connected world is like a complex ocean with swells, currents, and winds. And we are all stuck in the thick of it. Each condition can spell danger or opportunity and cannot be controlled. But you have the power to help your people navigate these choppy waters. The question is: Will you give them a raft or a sailboat?

THE RAFT

A client of mine appeared on maybe the most unnerving reality TV show ever. The premise: You float on a raft for a week in the Bermuda Triangle with a person chosen specifically to grate on your nerves.

Claustrophobia on the open seas!

A raft gives you no control. It just bobs along at the mercy of its surroundings until someone rescues you.

We live in an age of personalized automation, from Amazon recommendations to YouTube algorithms serving up the next video. Our desires, values, and focus are subject to vast aggregate trends and shopping histories. We trade control for convenience, reinforcing a system that rewards passivity and reactiveness.

We all live on this raft, at least part of the time. ("Surfing" the Internet is an ironic metaphor. It implies that we're riding waves of information—active, carefree, in control—when in truth they're crashing down on us.) And that can be okay. Amazon, for instance, is better at picking out gifts than my own family. Who knew I couldn't live without a loopy iPhone case? Amazon did.

Floating on a raft at work is far less benign.

Our friend Harry is digging into an important presentation. A colleague pops in with a question that takes 10 minutes. Then he takes a bathroom break—there goes that inhibitory spillover. Kidding, kind of. Just as Harry starts to refocus, an urgent e-mail arrives. Another 10 minutes gone.

He exhales, then loses himself in Facebook for 15 minutes. The first slide is almost done (yes!) when a meeting reminder pops up. Harry will have to finish his presentation at home after everyone's in bed.

He is busy, to be sure. But *reactive* will never be *productive*.

Harry is stuck on a raft.

THE SAILBOAT

Jack contends with the same ocean but navigates quite differently. Jack is on a sailboat.

Instead of helplessly succumbing to the wind, he harnesses its power with focus sails. Jack acts instead of reacting. He is focus-wise.

Before starting his own presentation, Jack puts a sign outside his office asking others to e-mail him with any needs, then closes the door. Next, he turns off the notifications on his smartphone and sets an autoreply telling colleagues to call with anything urgent. (He knows the world is less likely to call him than e-mail or text.)

Jack's cruising on his presentation when the meeting reminder pops up. He needs to go, but it's okay; he has arranged with his manager to stay for only the first 15 minutes. Besides, it'll give him a chance to catch a colleague with information vital to Jack's presentation—which he later finishes before 5.

Jack limits distraction in some areas and uses it to his advantage in others. He affects his environment in a way that inspires others to emulate him. Instead of drifting on a raft, he captains a sailboat.

Other, less productive employees look at Jack and think, "I wonder if he is using the same wind we are using." He is, but he is more focus-wise than those around him, so he can get to where he is going (a completed presentation) faster.

DROP THAT MARSHMALLOW

It would be impossible to overstate the importance of cultivating a sail mindset.

You've probably heard of the marshmallow test, a series of studies on delayed gratification in the late 1960s and early 1970s by psychologist Walter Mischel at Stanford University.[1] Children were offered one marshmallow now or two later if they could wait about 15 minutes.

Some kids ate the marshmallow as soon as the researchers left the room. Others resisted at first, smelling and touching the treat, but ultimately gave in. Still others managed to wait for the greater reward.

The test results proved more accurate than IQ in predicting SAT scores, drug and alcohol resistance, body mass index, and other life measures. The children who waited did better in all these areas.

What separated those who could resist from those who indulged? The winners kicked the table, pulled their hair, and even covered their eyes to neutralize the object of their desire. At first glance, this might seem like an example of kids simply distracting themselves, but the implications run far deeper. The differentiator between the successful and unsuccessful was not their willpower but rather their ability to take control of their attention. The marshmallow served as the tempting distraction keeping them from their goal. They put their attention in a more productive place as they shifted it away from the marshmallow. A child's version of the power of the sail mindset in action, something that proved to be of incalculable worth for the rest of their lives.

Jack, by the way, wanted to check his Facebook feed as much as Harry did. But he exercised the cognitive self-control to redirect his attention, ignoring the metaphorical marshmallow in the process. By resisting all the marshmallows around him, Jack claimed a greater reward: finishing his presentation at work so he could enjoy his evening.

Are you equipping your people to manage the endless supply of marshmallows in front of them? Or are they shoving as many as they possibly can in their mouths and playing Chubby Bunny all day?

ALLOCATING THE RIGHT FOCUS AT THE RIGHT TIME

To be focus-wise, we need to recognize that focus isn't one-size-fits-all. Some roles and venues require more of it, others less. Some tasks can even be done with the TV on (the murmur of golf *is* rather soothing).

Focus-wise workers know *what, when, where, and how much* it's appropriate to focus. The constantly connected workplace contains many layers. Let's look at a few of them.

Where and When

Different situations require different levels of focused effort. We need full focus for things like hard mental work, deep thinking, prioritizing, and engaged conversation because our brains aren't wired to think about two things at once. (Effective tools, including a focus vault where you can work undisturbed, will be discussed in later chapters.) During a deep conversation with your spouse, you would never turn on the basketball game and claim to be multitasking (unless you plan on that spouse becoming an ex-spouse).

Other moments require less focus, such as replying to routine e-mails or copying-pasting data into spreadsheets. Some of your employees can do these tasks with light distractions in the background (the same way you—and by you, I mean me—might listen to a favorite high fantasy novel possibly called *The Wheel of Time* while washing dishes).

As we learned in Chapter 4, pairing certain light tasks can actually boost retention (through inhibitory spillover). A handout I provide during speeches says that doodling can improve focus and memory by 30 percent. Try it sometime.

There are times when little to no focus is required (such as during happy hour). At other moments, speed and availability matter more.

For instance, if you handle flight bookings, being available during bad weather and responding quickly are more important than deep thinking.

Roles

Focus also differs depending on the role. I once audited an all-team quarterly meeting on a consulting project. Everyone was asked to "find a place of inefficiency that is costing you time and mental energy unnecessarily." An admin said he could save two hours a week if his boss would just take 20 minutes to format data differently.

Easy solution, right? Wrong.

His boss was a global thought leader who earned $50,000 per speech. The admin made $15 an hour—his job was to do everything, including inefficient tasks, to preserve the boss's attention resources.

Part of being focus-wise is understanding that not all roles are created equal. Often, the most focus-wise action you can take is to divide roles in such a way that some individuals are assigned to handle the interruptions. For instance, a recent client reorganized their tech department. Applying lean methodology, they divided the teams between application development and maintenance. The maintenance team's sole responsibility is to handle the unexpected emergencies that previously wreaked havoc across the entire department. Product developers now work without interruption. The overall attention resources of the organization are far more efficiently allocated when those who most need focused work are given it.

Scale

Sometimes I start a presentation by showing a close-up section of the Mona Lisa that looks like globs of paint. "Who would hang this on their wall?" I ask. I then zoom out to the proper perspective and a masterpiece emerges from the chaos.

Pixar cofounder Ed Catmull will at times remind his artists that they're putting their own Mona Lisa under a blanket when they spend days on a background setting for a three-second segment. No one will notice their masterpiece.

Knowing what level of focus is required for a given situation is another aspect of being focus-wise.

CHOICES AND CONSEQUENCES

Despite the advice of many self-help gurus, it is, in fact, impossible to work a full-time job, work out 10 hours a week, coach the kids' soccer team, serve on the church committee, and get a full night's sleep. We have to make choices on what we're going to spend our time and energy on.

One of my clients, JR Rosania, is a sponsored athlete, an 18 time Ironman triathlete, and one of the world's leading fitness trainers. To become elite, he used to train 6 hours a day—on top of his day job.

But JR's single-minded devotion had damaged a more important part of his life. His wife put it plainly: "JR, I need a husband, and our kids need their daddy."

The ensuing conversation between them changed his life. JR needed to understand the difference between being physically fit and having real health. He learned a hard but important lesson—hyperfocus in one area often means abject failure in others. Like an invasive plant in a fragile ecosystem, hyperfocus sucks up all available resources. Now he speaks to others about how to achieve true health.

Many of my other athlete clients are so hyperfocused that they struggle to manage even basic responsibilities. They oversleep, missing appointments. Bills go unpaid. They don't know how to prioritize because life has been reduced to *one* priority: professional success.

They could use a little of JR's hard-earned insight.

You can help your people achieve effective balance in the way they allocate their focus. To simplify without being simple. To focus while allowing for diversion. To be digitally connected without being addicted.

CHAPTER 6

The Four Elements of Focus

S o now we know that focus is a unique and precious resource, one that we can cultivate or sabotage by what tasks we do and how we choose to do them. We know that distraction can be a good thing and that there is a time for diversion, a time for deep focus, and a time for multitasking.

But our choice to focus or not doesn't happen in a vacuum. We are all subject to hidden factors that affect our ability to focus—factors that we can either harness (sailboat) or endure (raft). I call these factors the Four E's, and they will inform the strategies we discuss throughout the rest of this book.

ENERGY

Our energy levels affect our ability to focus. The less energy we have, the harder it is to focus. The longer we focus, the harder it is to maintain focus. This is a concept called ego depletion.[1] According to the theory, every decision you make makes the next more difficult, and every bit of energy you spend focusing intently on a task decreases the energy you'll have to focus on the next. Making yourself listen to Uncle George drone on, for instance, means you'll be too mentally exhausted to resist diving into Instagram for an hour. It gets harder to make good decisions over time.

That's why marathons, cycling competitions, and triathlons all start in the morning, even in the dead of winter. That's when endurance athletes have the most energy and, therefore, perform best.

Although not all of us are morning people, most of us tend to flag as the workday comes to an end. I've polled audiences over and over about what time of day it's toughest to stay focused:

First two hours of work—19 percent

Just before lunch—7 percent

The two hours after lunch—36 percent

Near the end of the workday—38 percent

See how many people lose focus toward the end of the day? This is ego depletion at work.

Focused attention is an energy exhaustive system. Although your brain is only about 2 percent of your body weight, it consumes 20 percent of your daily calories.[2] It's a hungry hungry hippo. That's why you feel ready to conquer the world after your bagel and latté but crave a nap later on. It's a glucose issue.

Our brains need energy to focus. It doesn't take much (about 25 grams of glucose in the bloodstream, a banana's worth).[3] But without steady energy, work becomes sloppy.

A fascinating study revealed when parole judges were more likely to grant freedom. At the start of the day and right after lunch, prisoners had a 65 percent chance for parole. That percentage crashed to almost zero just before lunch and at the end of the day.[4] The specific times they performed better and worse might not align with your daily energy patterns, or what we see from most workers. The nature of their work requires extended periods of intense focus without breaks to move around or grab a snack. What this tells us is how significantly our decision making and focus is enhanced or impaired based on our available energy resources. When tired or hungry, we seek shortcuts that include upholding the status quo (i.e., not granting parole).

The essential partner of glucose is sleep. Without enough of it, we struggle to focus and succumb more easily to distraction, which is also why the vast majority of those who say they can't work well in the morning probably just haven't gotten enough sleep. A lack of sleep, of course, hurts the bottom line.

The Centers for Disease Control and Prevention has declared inadequate sleep, which affects more than a third of American adults, a public health issue. The resulting economic losses total $411 billion a year.[5]

So how does our awareness of the impact of our energy and glucose levels affect how we work? Rising and subsequently shining is helped by smart scheduling. Allocate precious energy to your most mentally exhausting tasks first. Do that hefty proposal now, rote e-mail responses later. (As leaders, we can help by understanding and accommodating our people's peak efficiency times—a vital but often overlooked part of managing.)

Planning starts at home. The night before, for instance, set out your clothes and prepare lunch. That way, you preserve focus and energy in the morning (more on this in Section 6).

Another way to bank energy is to limit daily decisions. Warren Buffett eats a burger every day and plays bridge every night. Barack Obama wears the same suit. The fewer decisions you have to make, the more space you have for important ones.

ENVIRONMENT

Want to change what you focus on? Change your sightline.

I recently started the food-reset regimen Whole30—during Girl Scout Cookie season. Eliminating processed sugar was harder with Samoas or Do-si-dos on the kitchen counter, in plain sight.

Google tackled this issue with Project M&M, an experiment in which they moved the much-consumed candy from glass jars to opaque containers. They then filled the clear jars with dried figs, pistachios, and other healthy snacks.

The results surprised even the behavioral scientists who conducted the research: Over seven weeks, employees ate 3.1 million fewer calories from M&Ms in Google's New York office alone.[6]

What's in your sightline?

Your environment shapes your focus, whether you work in a cubicle, open office, penthouse corner suite, or at home (more on workspaces in Section 3). Our eyes seize on light and movement.

In a virtual environment, this can mean an incessant parade of buttons, pop-ups, and alerts beckoning us to click. One way to regain control is to change your home screen from inbox to calendar. Copernicus famously told the world that the sun was the center of the galaxy even though everyone still believed it was the earth. In the Copernican spirit, I say you should put your calendar at the center of your computer screen even though everyone else centers their world around the inbox. Why do this? E-mail cedes control of your day to others; the calendar restores you as the master of it. Take your priorities and assign time chunks to cover each one. Set your calendar, rather than your inbox or task list, as the primary screen on your computer, and watch your productivity soar to the stars.

Emotion

Not long ago, I was asked to address the top global leaders of a Fortune 25 company—a truly amazing opportunity. Unfortunately, the conference was scheduled two days before my wife was due with our second child. Less than amazing. This left quite the quandary: risk the missed business opportunity or risk missing my son's birth day?

So I did the only reasonable thing: I made her decide.

To my surprise, she encouraged me to go. After all, I had seen my first child being born. How different could it be? When the day arrived, I kissed her goodbye and flew to New York.

I don't need to tell any parent how I was feeling as I boarded the plane. It was a huge mistake. Although the speech went well, I was a wreck. I spent the whole time berating myself for leaving my wife and possibly missing the birth of my child.

Emotion drives attention.

What does this mean for leaders? If you want your people to be focused, you have to engage the parts of them that drive their focus. And that's their emotions.

The mantra of "it's just business" fails to heed this critical truth. How many successful bands, sports teams, and business partnerships have crumbled because people ignored each other's emotions? One sarcastic comment from a colleague and all the money in the world won't overcome the emotional hijack.

The pulse of a room affects everything. When a deal is negotiated, does someone feel robbed? Does everyone on your ad hoc committee get along? During a meeting, do team members have something else on their minds?

If your people don't care about something, they'll struggle to focus on it. That makes work difficult, especially in a world where 87 percent of workers already aren't actively engaged (as we discovered in Section 1.)

Cultivating focus within our employees is also about cultivating empathy within ourselves. For instance: Would a vital piece of news, good or bad, be better delivered in person than by e-mail?

EXPERIENCE

Past experiences shape focus. What you *have* focused on is what you *will* focus on.

Our brains are constantly changing through something called neuroplasticity. Whenever we learn or experience something new, a neural connection is formed. The more you do a task, the more your brain remembers how to do it again. That's autopilot in a nutshell.

The first time you drove, you might have hesitated with the ignition. Then came that squeamish jolt after the engine turned over, not to mention when you put the car in gear and lurched forward.

You probably don't even remember getting in your car this morning, backing out of the driveway, then gliding into traffic. Autopilot guided your hands and feet because your brain long ago memorized all the steps (though we can feel slight vertigo after realizing we got to the market without remembering seeing an actual green light).

It's a brilliant feature. Because we can make only so many active decisions, autopilot helpfully steps in.

Our habits dictate where we focus. And as we learn new habits, our highly adaptive brains start cementing them as "normal."

What does this mean at work? If our brains are wired to check our phones for stimuli, then we can't go long without craving a dopamine hit. In the same way, flipping back and forth between tasks makes our gray matter enjoy the novelty of it.

When we try to focus on a project, our brain shouts, "I can't pay attention anymore! Wouldn't it be cool to look at something else?"

But if we teach our brain to focus on one task for longer periods, it remembers and stops shouting. This is where focus really pays off. When we learn to focus in one sphere for a long time, expertise results.

Expertise is married to focus. And as we learned in Chapter 4, the more focused attention you give to a sphere, the more objects you can handle within that sphere. By this I don't mean the oft-quoted (and incorrect) 10,000-hour rule. Rather, expertise is achieved through intentional focus on a specific area within a sphere that then allows you to move onto other areas in that sphere once mastered. As Daniel Goleman writes regarding Anders Ericsson, the psychologist whose research spawned the 10,000-hour rule, "Hours and hours of practice are necessary for great performance, but not sufficient. How experts in any domain pay attention while practicing makes a crucial difference. For instance, in his much-cited study of violinists—the one that showed the top tier had practiced more than 10,000 hours—Ericsson found the experts did so with full concentration on improving a particular aspect of their performance that a master teacher identified."[7]

Experience builds our ability to manage multiple inputs. We aren't born experts. But through focused training and repetition, we can learn to make our object of focus more important than anything happening on Facebook or Instagram.

We've now outlined how the Four E's—energy, environment, emotion, and experience—affect our focus. In Section 3, we'll explore the kind of space, both mental and physical, that makes the focus-wise grade.

NOW THAT I HAVE YOUR ATTENTION . . .

For Section 2 reflection questions, summary video, and next step resources, please visit focuswise.com/book

SECTION THREE

FOCUS-WISE SPACE

CHAPTER 7

In Praise of Walls

L et's examine the common wall.

(Thrilling stuff, I know, but trust me, it's important.)

A wall serves two primary purposes:

- Distinguish one place from another
- Keep out things that don't belong

Or should I say a wall *served* two primary purposes?

Turn on just about any home remodeling show, and you'll see what I mean. The first thing they do is decide how many walls to knock down. Sledgehammer versus drywall is a growing spectator sport.

Today, we want open floor plans that allow us to interact with as much of our home as possible without changing chairs. We want to be able to watch the TV in the living room from the kitchen while still having a clear view of the kids playing in the backyard. Down with walls! (Except for the bathroom walls. Those walls stay.)

Walls are now an endangered species. And not just physical walls, but virtual walls as well.

The omnipresence of digital devices has eroded the important distinctions between places.

We go to the beach; we work (with Coronas, of course). We go to the mountains; we work (thanks to satellites). We go to Thanksgiving dinner; we work (because who wants to talk with Aunt Milly?). We go to work, and...we don't work. We're too busy booking that beach vacation. And—perhaps the most disturbing trend of all—the place more and more of us get the most work done is on the pot (walls!). Homes have become offices, offices homes, and cars pretty much everything. They're effectively all just one place now. Great for convenience. Disastrous for attention.

Connectivity knows no walls. We carry it in our pockets wherever we go. No zone in our Matrix is safe from the agents of distraction.

At the office, walls meant to delineate rooms and separate the workplace from the outside might as well meet the sledgehammer. Employees are endlessly immersed in a world that won't stop chattering. No barrier can stem the flow of communication and information.

Not all that long ago, surroundings dictated tasks. At the factory or office, you focused on work. At home, you focused on domestic life. That's how the brain likes it. We develop our habits in environmentally specific settings.

Our brains don't know what to do with the constantly connected workplace. It's time to restore environments that let us concentrate. It's time to bring back the walls.

ENVIRONMENTAL PROTECTION

Where you work determines how you work. In 2015, I listened to a well-known billionaire investor address a small group of young leaders. He emphasized the importance of making the office a place people want to be. "If you're going to spend most of your life here, you should invest in it," he said.

Surroundings shape work habits, good and bad. When you go to work at the same place every day and sit at the same desk, your brain, subconsciously and consciously, adapts itself to a pattern of thinking and acting. Neuroscientist Donald Hebb coined the phrase "neurons that fire together wire together" in 1949. To better understand this, think of how a beaten path develops in a grassy field. People follow the route of others rather than tromping through the high grass. It's easier. The brain forms neural connections when we have frequent, similar, or repeated experiences. Once those have been formed, we naturally use those pathways because it takes less energy than forming new ones.

Barriers to Distraction, Bridges to Focus

Murphy's Law also applies to attention: If people *can* interrupt, they *will* interrupt. The easier it is to reach you, the more likely that interruption will be trivial. You may start to believe that there are people whose entire job is figuring out how to keep you from getting work done. You are in charge of a major acquisition. Now, it seems, you are in charge of deciding where to buy the cake for the monthly office birthday celebration as well. Think about the last time you struggled for traction on a project because of repeated intrusions. Did your employees know you needed to focus? Did you mitigate distracting technology?

And if this happens to you, it also happens to your team.

Sometimes it's our job as leaders to be interrupted (pitching in on last-minute projects, for instance). But we can also be blind to our own part in the cycle. In the absence of barriers, we might not perceive the cost to our people's resources when we delegate or check in excessively. A primary and extremely important part of leadership is to facilitate great work. Because access is so readily available to our teams, it can become easy to forget they often need us to get out of the way (even if we just have that one quick question).

Barriers are the only way to stem interruption. People often ask questions when they know the answers. They want approval, but they don't need it. They want to avoid responsibility, but they need to take it. Being unavailable frees you up to do the things you need to do and forces others to use their own judgment, becoming less dependent on you in the process.

This might mean retreating to an unreachable place for a time to focus on our most important tasks. I call this the "vault" (which we'll discuss in Chapter 9). We can also create digital barriers against texts, e-mails, alerts, and anything else that smartphones and computers can throw at us.

Focus begins with walls, both literal and figurative.

The key is to have distinct places. At your desk. In the break room. Out to lunch. In your car. On the sofa. In the bathroom (no YouTube in there without headphones, please). For leaders, it's imperative to create

a culture for the team that both imposes and respects these proverbial walls.

The late missionary Jim Elliot said, "Wherever you are, be all
there." Words to live, and work, by.

MENTAL SPACE

More than 300 years ago, Blaise Pascal invented the calculator,
providing the conceptual framework for the computer. He seemed
to presuppose our age of distraction and the constantly connected
workplace in two quotes:

"I have often said that the sole cause of man's unhappiness is that
he does not know how to stay quietly in his room."

"Distraction is the only thing that consoles us for miseries, and
yet it is itself the greatest of our miseries."

Without space, our priorities become muddled and distractions
seduce us. When did you last take time to press pause and just think?
The greater the noise, the greater the need for solitude.

So why do we spend so much energy fighting space? We don't
like it.

Most of us understand the perils of too much noise and stimu-
lation. But that doesn't necessarily compel us to do anything about
it. Our brains become wired for noise; cutting it off can spur with-
drawal symptoms. And those off-the-wagon cat video binges are
not pretty.

Tim Wilson of the University of Virginia studied the degree to
which people resist the solitude of their own thoughts.[1] In the first
round of tests, subjects struggled with just 6 to 15 minutes of quiet,
cheating by picking up a device or book.

The next rounds were shocking. Literally.

Given his subjects' propensity for distraction, Wilson provided
access to an uncomfortable one: a small electric jolt from a 9-volt bat-
tery. Two-thirds of the men resorted to shocking themselves rather

than letting their minds wander (just a quarter of the women did, so you can draw your own conclusions from that).

Pascal was right: Men, in particular, don't like to sit quietly.

That's a tragedy. Wandering minds are linked to increased creativity and better working memory[2]—the part of our brains that can help process the noise and information that bombards us every day.

But even if we understand the need for more mental space, how do we find the discipline to create it?

In Praise of Contemplation

My family once unplugged for a month. No TV, movies, digital music, smartphones—nothing that wasn't required for school or work. At first, we went out of our minds.

Then our brains began to adapt. We rewired them for talking instead of texting, reading books instead of scanning social media feeds, hiking instead of watching TV.

I have never been so engaged in my life. Research cited by the *Harvard Business Review* explains why: "Recent studies are showing that taking time for silence restores the nervous system, helps sustain energy, and conditions our minds to be more adaptive and responsive to the complex environments in which so many of us now live, work, and lead," write Justin Talbot-Zorn and Leigh Marz.[3] Cultivating silence and letting our minds wander opens us to novel ideas and information.

Here are a few key areas you must intentionally practice to cultivate mental space. We'll call them the Three P's.

Pause. Mark Rampolla, the founder of ZICO Beverages, is a friend and a client. Mark did something most entrepreneurs only dream of—he created a new market. Today, coconut water seems ubiquitous, but Mark is the one who started it all. Coconut water is now an $8 billion industry, and his business was so successful that the Coca-Cola Company bought it. He cites the discipline of *thought time* as one of the biggest secrets behind his success.

Inspired by his father-in-law, a neuroscientist who devotes whole days to thought time, Mark tried for once a week to pause and think from 3 PM until the end of the day. No phone, Internet, or even books. Nothing but a piece of paper.

At first, thought time became nap time. But eventually this discipline spurred new ideas and solutions to business problems. Mark credits many of his successful ZICO decisions to the space he gave himself simply to think. (Bill Gates, by the way, will spend two weeks straight in thought time. Seems to have worked out for him.)

Focus doesn't happen in one sitting, and the time and method will vary from person to person. For me, it includes prayer and silence. Another good practice is called *mindfulness*—focusing your awareness on the present moment. (I like the Headspace app for this.) Whatever you call it, just 10 minutes a day has been shown to dramatically increase the ability for sustained focus.

Another key element of pausing is to *mind the gaps*. In the London Subway, there's a sign to remind you to step back so you don't get run over. Mentally, we need to step back and mind the gaps between the different events, roles, and spheres of our lives so we don't get run over by those as well.

This means planning your day so you're not dashing from event to event. The frustration of one meeting, for instance, can bleed into the next, depriving your mind of the time it needs to close and open again. Press pause for a few minutes between obligations, and give your mind the space it needs to reset.

We need the same kind of pauses at home. My wife used to let my kids open the garage door to greet me when I got home from work. Aside from the danger of a 2-year-old running up to my car, there was the issue of mental space.

Eventually, we agreed that Dad needed to sit behind the wheel to clear his head before he could be fully present for a rousing game of chase the 2-year-old. It's amazing what 2 minutes of clearing my head of the day's work and reminding myself to jump into the next sphere fully will do for my ability to be present with the people I love.

Prepare. Through preparation and visualization, Sun Tzu writes in *The Art of War,* battles are won before they're fought.

Take a few minutes at the start of the day to plan, then extend the habit to everything from meetings to presentations. I call this practice *isolation before collaboration.* It's amazing how much is wasted by people jumping into meetings without having done their own thought work prior.

For instance, preparing your thoughts and remarks before you jump into a meeting, conversation, or presentation can have a huge impact on the effectiveness of your words. People think great communicators are capable of effectively talking off the cuff. Nothing could be further from the truth. Sure, some nonverbal communication habits can make certain people more capable of capturing the attention of the room, but to be truly effective, ideas require space so you can structure them for maximize impact. A preacher friend I know practices his weekly sermon three times from the stage on which he'll give it. In the process, he refines and hones it down to a powerful message. Of course, the congregation assumes he's a "natural."

Another good practice is to prepare your workday before diving in. In today's world, if you don't intentionally create space to prepare your day, you will be the raft rather than the sail. Even something as simple as reviewing your to-do list and prioritizing the top two to three tasks you absolutely have to get done today will help you realize a generous spike in productivity (more on this in Section 6).

Process. At the end of a project, a meeting, and the workday itself, we need time to pull back and ask: Why is this important, and what have I learned?

Researchers found that call-center employees who spent 15 minutes at the end of the day contemplating what they had learned performed 23 percent better after 10 days than colleagues who didn't reflect.[4]

Journaling is one way to do this. Sometimes I'll simply write "What I learned today" at the top of the screen and jot down a few bullets:

- A new slide would bring home point no. 3

- Need a survey of how many CEOs use lockout tools for vault time

- Frenchies actually make good pets (if I write it enough, it will be true)

Walls—both mental and physical—give us the space to be our best.

CHAPTER 8

Office Space

T he words *office space* conjure up the iconic 1999 movie of the same name. The phrase has become shorthand for a dystopia of uninspiring work, firings (or "downsizing" as we were saying back then), and cubicles.

The history behind Peter and the gang's work environment has many twists and contradictions. Office spaces have at different times been symbols of hierarchy, liberation, and soul-crushing uniformity. Today, most space design is driven far more by cost and wow factor than anything else. In fact, a recent executive survey revealed that minimizing distractions was the lowest consideration when designing office space.[1]

Those executives might change their minds if they knew that, according to one study, only 7 *percent* of workers say they're most productive at the office.[2]

It's high time to change that. We can start by considering the pros and cons of each work setting.

OPEN OFFICE

Background

Open offices emerged when Frank Lloyd Wright and other architects in the early twentieth century dismissed walls and rooms as fascist and confining.[3] They wanted to liberate employees. The idea was a rejection of corporate hierarchy that was patterned after the military (put in your time, get your corner office). Companies altered this vision of liberated workers by packing in as many as they could. The open office, with its extended rows of desks, was born.

The open office has come back with a vengeance in the twenty-first century. Perhaps most famously, Facebook in 2015 expanded into a 430,000-square-foot building designed by Frank Gehry. It fits 2,800 employees, including CEO Mark Zuckerberg, who sits among the ranks.[4]

Egalitarian? Maybe, but the real draw for companies mimicking Silicon Valley is cost savings. Walls, doors, and even cubicles are more expensive than rows of desks. Today, almost 70 percent of U.S. employees work in open offices.[5]

Pros

Open offices can nurture productivity through a shared mission. Consultant Andrew Challenger told Bloomberg that they "cultivate a cohesive and collaborative culture and stymie unproductive behavior. If your coworkers can see your computer screens and hear your phone calls, you'll be less likely to peruse Facebook, online shop, or make personal calls."[6] Furthermore, a "self-policing" atmosphere motivates employees to come in on time and stay until close.

Zuckerberg didn't build an empire on stupid decisions. Although Facebook may not be as egalitarian as its open office suggests, the fact that he sits among his employees sends a message: Everyone's contributions matter.

An open floor plan "enables better collaboration, which we think is key to building the best services for our community," Zuckerberg told *Business Insider*.[7]

Cons

Noise, noise, and noise. A survey of workers by the University of Sydney found a "lack of sound privacy" to be their number one distraction. And "the loss of productivity due to noise distraction…was doubled in open-plan offices compared to private offices," the study's authors said, citing prior research.[8] There's a quick lesson to be learned here: No one likes the loud talker. Sorry not sorry if that's you.

The critiques of the open office are many, including lack of overall privacy; inability to scale, forcing teams with different work processes to share space; and poor accommodation for introverts.[9]

A large Canadian oil-and-gas company shifting from a traditional office to an open design hired University of Calgary psychologists to gauge employee satisfaction 4 weeks and then 6 months in.[10] The researchers asked about stress level, job performance, and relationships.

"The employees suffered according to every measure: The new space was disruptive, stressful, and cumbersome, and, instead of feeling closer, coworkers felt distant, dissatisfied, and resentful," Maria Konnikova writes in *The New Yorker*. "Productivity fell."

A colleague and friend of mine, Mike Maddock, tried switching his creative team to a fully open office floor plan. It seemed like a big win. They were even spotlighted in a Chicago newspaper for the innovation. Unfortunately, that news wasn't fit to print. Within a year, two-thirds of the team had left thanks to the increases in distraction. Here's what he said about the experience:

> At the insistence of a team member, we recently retried the open concept in a small part of our office, which we titled "The Collaboratorium." It immediately became a stage for the primary proponent of the idea. He lectured, munched crunchy foods, and bedazzled anyone who would give him attention. All that was missing was a spotlight. Headphones became necessary for everyone within earshot. He no longer works at our company, nor do the two people who sat closest to him. Coincidence? Probably not.

Is employee unhappiness and the subsequent drop in productivity worth the money saved by having an open office?

CUBICLES

Background

Cubicles, partitioned spaces organically grouped, were conceived in the 1950s as an attempt to humanize the white-collar assembly line.[11] The U.S. furniture company Herman Miller added larger surfaces and multiple desk heights in the mid-1960s. Their popularity with organizations surged in the 1980s and 1990s amid the frenzy of mergers, buyouts, and layoffs. Besides being cheaper than walls, cubicles have a significant tax benefit: They are furniture that businesses can deduct after 7 years (walls, as permanent structures, require 39 years to depreciate).[12] Accounting departments love this kind of write-off.

Today's cubicles can be assembled, disassembled, and adjusted with little fuss. They're not offices, nor are they the open-desk farms of yore. They're in between, like the middle-management class that emerged with them.

Pros

In the absence of a private office, cubicles fit part of the bill for cultivating mental space. Their surfaces and wall-style barriers can be personalized for a sense of continuity. And though cubicles don't block noise, they can be adjusted to filter out some visual distraction.

Furthermore, *Office Space* and *Dilbert* cartoons notwithstanding, cubicles aren't just the province of worker bees. Some leaders, echoing Facebook, occupy cubicles to be closer to their people. This can foster a more egalitarian atmosphere while also providing a firsthand look at areas that might need improvement.

Cons

Back to noise. Like open offices, cubicles leave employees at the mercy of loud neighbors (again, don't be the loud talker), piped-in music, and meetings conducted in the open. *Office Space* is almost a documentary when it comes to cataloging the distractions of noise.

Cubicles also tend to be deprived of windows and natural light. "Natural lighting," Jeff Pochepan writes in *Inc.*, "not only affects how well we are able to see, but it can also boost our mood, energy level, and hormonal balance."[13] Artificial or poor lighting can raise stress levels and hamper focus.

And don't forget that many employees who work in a cubicle describe their environment as a "cubicle farm." This isn't an endearing term used because their office space reminds them of simpler times when they were on their grandpappy's farm. People working in this environment are more likely to view themselves as sheep as opposed to productive, and unique, members of your team.

WORKING REMOTELY

Background

Expanded Internet access allows our people to work around the corner or around the world, providing unprecedented flexibility and potential savings on overhead.

And employees like it too.[14] Sixty-five percent of workers said telecommuting would make them more efficient than going to an office. Among their top reasons:

- Fewer colleague interruptions (76 percent)
- Fewer distractions (75 percent)
- Fewer meetings (69 percent)
- Less office politics (68 percent)
- Reduced commuting stress (67 percent)
- A more comfortable working environment (51 percent)

Interestingly, some of distraction's bugaboos—texting, IM, and phone calls—become lifelines when you can't literally tap an employee on the shoulder.

Pros

Employees who work remotely can more easily create a vault for optimal focus. Noise and other distracting stimuli are neutralized when other people aren't dictating the environment.

Telecommuters also free themselves from the cultural need to waste time while looking productive. Any company monitoring feels more helpful than intrusive from a distance.

Lastly, self-starters can do especially well if their leaders are vigilant about staying connected. A solid relationship with the team, wherever it is, goes a long way toward making telecommuting successful.

Cons

Accountability may be the biggest issue. How can you tell how much someone is working, other than the work she sends and the occasional conference call and meeting? And without the chance of someone walking by and seeing their screen, there is nothing discouraging constant use of social media.

Remote workers can also become socially disconnected from their teams. Without the regular connection of a break room or water cooler, leaders have to work harder to interact with their nonoffice people. One manager I know uses FaceTime with his remote employee in the team's morning meeting. It's a small but significant gesture of connection.

And a vault at home (or the library or coffee shop) isn't always easy to maintain. Personal and professional lines can blur for remote workers. How does anyone focus on a crucial call when his kids are begging him to play? (see Figure 8.1) (Seriously, if you can help me here, please message me.)

THE FOCUS-WISE SPACE

Whatever you think of open-office, cubicle, or remote-work settings, the reality is that the leaders utilizing these options in the workplace typically don't make focus the priority they should. How can we change that? By creating space with function and focus in mind.

Most companies give lip service to the need for focus spaces, but they often provide so few of them that no employee feels like they can use them. If there are two available for every 50 people, you might as well have none. When they do use them, the rooms often

Figure 8.1   This is where I found my son after taking a water break while working on this book. Yes, my keyboard is from 1985.

become areas for personal calls instead of work. And if that's their association, the spaces will be largely ignored. If people assume you aren't working in a focus space, then why would anyone in their right mind use it?

Reduce the Noise

All open floor plans are not created equal. The more people you can see and the more sounds you can hear from your workstation, the more likely you are to be interrupted.

Visual. Every object in your field of view is an opportunity to divert your attention or have it diverted. As we discussed in Chapter 6, if you want to eat fewer Girl Scout Cookies, don't set a box on the counter. In much the same way, aim to reduce the field of view. Segment, a data analytics company, suffered from the consequences of an open warehouse. CEO Peter Reinhardt explained the situation like this: "These long lines of sight across the workspace, where you have people you know and recognize moving by and talking to each other.

It was incredibly distracting."[15] They solved this problem by choosing a new location with a more labyrinth-like setup where walls, corners, and even plants limit line of sight.

Even if you have no control over the overall design of the workspace, do what you can to set up your seating arrangement with the goal of keeping people out of your natural line of sight.

Audio. In much the same way, take simple steps to reduce the noise of your space. Glossed concrete and hardwood floors might look great, but they reflect sound. Choose your flooring, furniture, and even office equipment with an ear toward the noise they will create or eliminate. Select space with sound-dampening walls.

Match the Space to the Task

Think of exclusive airline lounges. They're modular, featuring premium chairs, desks, work areas, private rooms, and charging stations for every device. You select where to sit based on your particular focus needs at that moment. And you can change when your needs change. If I have hard work to knock out that requires full focus, I'm finding a private cubicle. If it's been a long day at work, I'm headed to the bar to watch TV, talk with fellow travelers, and occasionally knock out a few medium-focus, basic e-mails.

As leaders, we can do the same thing for our people. We can create a variety of spaces rather than imposing a one-size-fits-all scheme, says Mike McKeown, a workplace design expert at Gensler, the world's largest workplace design firm.

Employees have diverse space needs based on the variety and focus demands of their work. Some are rarely or never in the office and may not require assigned seating. Others need the continuity of their own desk and may rely more heavily on office services or support spaces. And then there are anchors: administrative and support staff who sit in the same spot so colleagues can find them. Most of us have a variety of tasks that demand different levels of focus and can benefit from a variety of spaces throughout the day. When planning space it is important not to make too many assumptions or generalize the nature of focus work. Gaining a deeper understanding of how people work allows us to create more specific work style profiles and design the physical environment more effectively.

Sometimes team members need a place to collaborate, whereas other times solitary focus is required. An isolated space can serve for hunkering down and getting focused work done. Another area can offer subtle distractions amid tedious work. As we discussed in Section 2, we can benefit from inhibitory spillover. Background noise can actually stimulate our focus when the work alone doesn't exactly create the mental challenge necessary to generate what Hungarian psychologist Mihály Csíkszentmihályi terms *flow*, or being in the zone. And of course, there's the space designated for Friday afternoon margaritas (team-building without ziplines).

When people move around, retention increases. But our brains don't just respond to new stimuli; they like habits too. Tasks associated with a specific environment become second nature when we enter that environment.

I do my deep thinking on the patio.

I write case studies in this room.

I file reports at this desk.

Although most every company that uses the open-office concept claims to have a multifunctional design, the truth is few actually create the balance, ease of access, and utility to make it useful.

A 2013 Gensler survey revealed that innovative companies are five times more likely to balance group and individual workspaces. The ratio was 44 percent open office and 45 percent private; the least innovative organizations had a 60:30 ratio.[16]

I've seen companies design places with portable walls that can be rearranged to meet the needs of a particular day. Variety and flexibility are key, as is functionality.

Tackle the Barriers to Entry

McKeown encourages his clients to recognize practical barriers to usage. Along with providing a variety of spaces, it is also crucial to align proper technology and support services to make the experience as effective as possible. He says, for instance, that employees shunned company-provided spaces because the login and Wi-Fi were cumbersome and not seamless to work flow.

Another challenge with offices that allow their people to rotate through different workspaces is that some people have a need to create a sense of place. Where do the *Star Wars* action figures go if you don't have your own desk?

There are two ways to adjust for this. First, for those who have a strong desire to make a particular space their own, give it to them. But the better plan is to recognize the deeper need. People long for something that tells them that this location where they spend the majority of their waking hours also physically embodies who they are. It's distinct, personalized, and them. One way you can accomplish this is modeled by my client, Westwood Holdings, a publicly traded financial investment firm based in Dallas. Rather than fill their walls with expensive original works of art, they fill their walls with framed photos of employee vacations and community service projects. They also have a wall in the various break rooms where photos are added frequently.

It all starts with listening to your people. Ask what would help make them most productive. Employee choice is critical for buy-in—even if everyone's wish list isn't fulfilled.

In the next chapter, we'll explore another crucial part of cultivating mental space: the vault. And the buy-in starts with you.

CHAPTER 9

The Vault

Remember writing term papers in college? Maybe you were responsible and started a week or so prior to the due date. Or maybe you pounded it out the day before the deadline. Everyone has a system (if we can call procrastination a system).

My question is: *Where* did you typically write your papers?

Your dorm room?

The library?

Starbucks?

It always intrigues me where people go when they really need to concentrate and get something accomplished. When that term paper is due, most students flee their normal surroundings and seek a spot without distractions. They probably populate their favorite coffee shop, drowning out their environment with headphones.

Where do *you* go today?

As I write this, I'm sitting in my backyard. It has a small covered patio with plush outdoor furniture, and my favorite chair faces a perimeter of trees and a manicured lawn. When serious work needs to get done, this is where I sit.

It's early, so the Dallas heat hasn't set in. Some traffic noise reaches me, but mostly all I hear are birds and the occasional bark of my neighbor's dog. The only distraction is a squirrel scurrying around an oak in search of food.

My phone is in the house. In an emergency, my wife will get me. Otherwise, the only message that could reach me would have to come from a carrier pigeon.

The backyard patio is my vault. I'll get more done here in an hour than most of my colleagues will accomplish all day.

Modern workplaces don't provide quiet places of concentration. As a result, our attention grows weaker by the day. This isn't just inconvenient—it's tragic. Exceptional work requires space to focus.

Where can you and your team go to harness attention?

John Kim, a top investor in New York, manages the wealth of the superrich. In a world where speed is everything, he blocks out more than an hour a day each morning to read and contemplate questions such as, "What will the world look like in 5 years?"

There's perhaps no industry that feels more obligated to stay on top of up-to-the-second data than financial investing. There are even books written about investment desks who benefit from split-second advantages in data (e.g., *Flash Boys: A Wall Street Revolt*, by Michael Lewis). What happens if one of John's investments crashes from an announcement? When everyone else has already pulled their stock, he will lose millions in the hour he takes to make a move! John understands what few others do—the advantage of the day goes not to the one who reads the newest CNBC update 30 seconds faster but instead to the one who sees the world more clearly.

John has a degree from Harvard and a PhD in economics from MIT, but the truth is, as he would attest, it doesn't take a genius to know how to create unique value in today's world. It takes creating the space to think when no one else is.

Many of us would protest, "I don't have an hour a day!" But John beats the market because he does what few others will.

The interesting thing is that people like John used to be the norm. Now, in today's hyperconnected world, they are the exception. It's like my grandfather, who was in great shape but never worked out at a gym. The demands of his job and life kept him in motion. You don't need to run on a treadmill when you are moving all day long.

Today, we go to gyms because our jobs leave us stationary. The irony is that there is nothing in a gym that we can't get for free somewhere else. We have the equivalent of pull-up bars (trees), free weights (furniture), and treadmills (the sidewalk) in abundance. We go to gyms because they are distinct places set apart for something we need that our stationary lifestyle doesn't naturally give us.

Unfortunately, in today's day and age, we seem to have no equivalent for our attention health. No place to burn the fat of distraction, exercise our imaginations, and build up muscle memory for focused attention.

A GYM FOR YOUR MIND

But each of us *can* have a focus gym. It's your vault, and it helps preserve attention and keep unwanted distractions—human and digital—away from you. In this chapter, you'll learn how to build it.

A component of my work involves helping often resistant leaders create vaults for themselves. Then they can evangelize the concept for their employees.

What does a vault look like?

It's *an unreachable place where you go for defined periods to focus on your most important tasks*. The location can be anywhere from a home office to even a cubicle. Here are some tips to help you and your people create a vault in any environment.

Keep the Door Closed

An effective vault separates you from everyone else. Save your open-door policy for nonvault time. Your employees will live.

If you have a cubicle or open-office desk, try to adopt a conference room as your vault. If real walls aren't available, build virtual ones.

When settling in on a plane, I'll chat with my seatmate. Then comes the international signal that I'm busy: "It was nice meeting you," I'll say, before opening my laptop and slipping on noise-canceling headphones. My virtual door stays shut, and I get heaps of work done.

Invest in Noise-Canceling Headphones

If you don't have a door to close or your walls are thin, headphones are a great help. Not only do they block out noise, but they also tell others, "I'm blocking out noise for a reason." Headphones isolate you from the world (is it possible to be a teenager without them?).

But there are two important caveats for you and your people.

Set Ground Rules. Corporate leaders often complain to me about the sight of headphones on their young employees. But their real irritation is reserved for workers who wear them all day.

As leaders, we need to train our people to use headphones for specific periods of focus, then otherwise put them away. If headphones are a default, they lose their value.

You should also establish a policy for how and when people can interrupt each other during headphone use. Is a shoulder tap okay, or would an IM be better? No one likes to be yanked out of the zone, but sometimes it's necessary.

Headphones Aren't Always Helpful. They only help if they block out noise rather than adding to it. Audiobooks, podcasts, and music with words that you can't ignore steal attention. These are not light-focus activities (see Chapter 4). Anything with words requires your active attention to process. The vault is for full-focus work. Keep the pairings to tasks that enhance your attention. Headphones are most effective when they play white noise, instrumental music, or . . . nothing.

Hang Up a Do Not Disturb Sign

Make sure every member of your team has a clear sign to hang where others can't miss it. And there's no rule against creativity:

- Do not disturb: Really. I need an hour.

- Please e-mail or leave me a voicemail.

- Pretty sure I have a flesh-eating virus.

- Wrong door!

Hang it on your door, across the opening to your cubicle, or tape it to the back of your chair. Unnecessary interruptions will cease.

In fact, I was asked about do not disturb signs so many times that I finally had a designer create one: DO NOT DISTURB—IN MY VAULT. I've had several clients buy these signs for everyone in their company. Those signs have profoundly changed the cubicle culture in those companies.

Disconnect

A closed door and Do Not Disturb sign aren't always enough. Sometimes the person most likely to distract you is *you*.

Turn off your Wi-Fi and phone service. (If you need a connection for work, simply switch off everything that can interrupt you.) You can go an hour or two without e-mails, texts, and social media. In fact, you'll work with more efficiency and less stress. A University of California at Irvine study reveals that without e-mail, people multitask less and focus longer[1] (big surprise). Stress, measured by heart rate variability, was lower too.

If those options aren't working for you, invest in an application that forces you to shut off the world. I use one that requires me to totally reboot my computer if I want to get back online. And in case it wasn't already obvious: Turn off your phone (for tools, see Chapter 11). Lock it away if you must.

If a laptop is necessary in your vault, try limiting yourself to the screen in which you're working. A full-screen view will keep your eyes from wandering. It's a small sacrifice for focus and exponentially increased productivity.

FORMING THE VAULT HABIT

Now it's time to train your mind to recognize your vault as sacred and distraction-free. A vault should unequivocally say, "This is where I work." Below are tips to help you and, in turn, your team.

The Ideal Vault Is the Same Place Every Day

By committing to one workspace, you'll form habits that boost your productivity and make you an asset in an attention-deprived world. If, as with me, the same spot every day leads to boredom and a *loss* of productivity, you can alternate among a few places. Just make sure any space you use provides complete privacy from the people who would interrupt you if they could see you—no interruptions allowed!

Just keep the deeper principle in mind: When you enter a vault, your brain needs to automatically kick into work mode.

It's Only for Work

It's not for checking e-mail, reading novels, or monitoring stocks. Your vault is the one place reserved solely for work. Simple as that.

Leave It When the Session Is Done

This means getting up and walking somewhere else to check Facebook. Your vault is where you form productive habits. If you play there, your brain becomes confused.

Reward yourself when vault time is over. Get coffee, chat with an employee, or dive headlong into whatever enticement our shared Matrix has to offer.

This is the time when your team can reach you again. Employees will quickly become used to your being unreachable during vault time—especially if they're cultivating their own vault habits.

Treat yourself to some endorphins by checking off vault time from your calendar. You might also write down what you accomplished in your sanctuary.

If You Can't Leave the Vault, Transform It

If you can't physically leave your office, then undo all the things you did to make it a vault. Open your door, take off the Do Not Disturb sign, and turn your phone back on. You can transform your office or cubicle from workspace back to everything-else space.

Get Your Community to Buy in

The vault works only if those who want to reach you know when and why you are not available. On the other hand, you don't want to interrupt 30 people with an announcement that focus is too important to be interrupted.

I make sure two people always know when I'm entering my vault: my wife and my director of operations. My wife can then serve as a deflection for any personal interruptions, my ops director for all work-related ones. The rest can figure it out. This is particularly important early on when you are trying to establish a new habit, you need people working to support your habit rather than trying to break the proverbial vault code to ask you about the football game from last night.

In Section 3, we've celebrated walls, physical and virtual, as a way to create focus-wise space. In the next section, we'll take a deeper dive into how to make technology actually work for you and your people.

Now That I Have Your Attention ...

For Section 3 reflection questions, summary video, and next step resources, please visit focuswise.com/book

FOCUS-WISE TECHNOLOGY

CHAPTER 10

Relationship Status: It's Complicated

W ith a deadline for a project last approaching, I decided recently it was time to "disconnect." Thirty-six hours—no social feeds, no e-mail, no entertainment media.

Finally, some time away from the scourge of modern technology.

Except that during that time, I used the Web for controlled bouts of research. And typed on my laptop. And listened to my "focus" playlist through noise-canceling headphones on a flight (nullifying the nontech distraction of a screaming baby).

THANK GOD FOR THE GIFT (?!) OF MODERN TECHNOLOGY

Technology is ever more powerful, ubiquitous, and maddening when it doesn't work. The modern workplace has a love-hate relationship with technology. It's the cause and the cure of our problems. It's a panacea, and it's a plague. It can increase productivity and boost the bottom line, but it can also be hard to adopt and a huge distraction for employees.

As leaders, our job is to maximize the benefits while minimizing the downsides. The lack of technology frustrates many workers. According to one survey, 89 percent of employees feel deprived of the latest technology.[1] At the same time, employees don't feel equipped to handle the distractions tech creates. In an Oxford Economics study, just 41 percent of employees said they had the necessary tools to block out distractions in the workplace. Sixty-three percent of executives, on the other hand, thought the opposite.[2]

Despite these frustrations, it doesn't seem to be due to a lack of trying. In 2016, nearly nine out of 10 businesses actively invested in an initiative to make their workplace more digital.[3] The commitment is there, but too often the hidden and complex implications are ignored, leaving money invested while unintended consequences abound.

Our love–hate relationship with technology can be summarized in three paradoxes.

Paradox 1: We Want to Be Accessible But Need Boundaries to Stay Sane

Twentieth-century philosopher Martin Heidegger spoke of technology as "the summoning of everything into assured availability."[4] Perhaps he should have summoned only *most* things.

Technology opens a floodgate that lets everything in—whether we want it at that particular moment or not.

It's the conduit for our professional *and* personal lives. On vacation, you want your phone to take pictures and preserve memories. But it's still spitting out work e-mails and meeting alerts that nag at you. Conversely, you feel pressure to ignore personal texts at work (at least until no one is looking). E-mail provides easy access but can also choke our inboxes. The same tools create both efficiency and inefficiency.

Paradox 2: We Want to Focus But Need to Be Interrupted by What Matters More Than What We're Doing in the Moment

Electronic interruption is bad when wasteful but helpful when urgent or otherwise important. Fifteen texts analyzing your fantasy league are a hindrance at work. One text saying a client is about to bail might help you prevent disaster.

Paradox 3: We Want to Disconnect But Fear We Will Miss Out

Then there's the fear of missing out, or FOMO. For a leader, this could mean the urge to interrupt your people with frequent check-ins. Tech can somehow make leading versus micromanaging even tougher to navigate.

These paradoxes result in some challenging dynamics in our corporate, team, and consumer cultures—and more than enough blame to go around.

TECHNOLOGY MEETS CULTURE

Human beings are usually at the heart of distractions. Not just the loud guy in the next cubicle or that crying baby on my flight. Marketers target us with ads and alerts for their products, colleagues e-mail questions and demands, and friends and family text about tee times and when we'll be home for dinner.

These interruptions aren't a tech problem. They're a cultural one.

Organizations face their own cultural challenges. Sometimes the technology in place works fine but isn't being used properly. Sometimes it needs upgrading, but change-averse leadership instead piles bad tech on top of bad tech. Employees themselves can feel wedded to a certain technology or complain about changes they had no voice in shaping. People can be opinionated, obstinate, and unpredictable and deliberately try to subvert what otherwise would have been a welcome technological change.

And those people are probably (generally) well-intentioned. What happens when they're not?

TECHNOLOGY MEETS GREED

Business technology aims to drive engagement so that businesses will prosper. Many of us want to make Silicon Valley the villain—perhaps a subtler version of the Matrix monster feeding on our distraction.

And why not? A lot of tech is practically designed for addiction, as Adam Alter explains in *The Guardian*.[5] This is the same force at work that addicts people to slot machines. It's called intermittent reinforcement, a concept first revealed during the 1950s in an experiment by B.F. Skinner.[6] He put hungry rats in a box with a lever. In one setting, a food pellet would drop out when the rat hit the lever. This rat quickly learned it had a constant source of food and nourishment. So, it enjoyed life, exercised on its wheel, and accessed a pellet whenever it pleased. Another box didn't dispense pellets at all. This rat also lived a healthy life, never paying any mind to the useless lever. It ran on its wheel, slept, and searched for food elsewhere. Yet another box intermittently dispersed pellets. Sometimes a pellet would drop out when the rat hit the lever. Other times... nothing. Sometimes the rat would hit the lever 10 times before a pellet came out. This poor rat became so neurotic that it wasted its entire existence hitting the lever, in fear of missing out. It didn't run on its wheel, and sometimes it didn't even leave the lever to go drink water. Many of these rats died of exhaustion or starvation. The inconsistent and unpredictable reward is what creates the addiction. Just as gamblers do with slot machines, we invest a lot of time and energy into our tech. To walk away from it means we would lose everything we invested. When we get even the smallest of rewards, it reinforces our addiction, causing us to invest even more—just like a gambler after winning a few shiny quarters.

Social media has created a new category of addiction. Ongoing interaction on social media often elevates the production of both oxytocin and dopamine, "mimicking what happens when we have a drug addiction." Compulsive Facebook users share some of the same brain patterns as gambling or drug addicts, according to a sobering study in the journal *Psychology Reports*.[7]

And this is just one of many psychological triggers that tech companies employ to keep the attention of their customers. Gamers, including children, are enticed to continue uninterrupted for just 99 cents or to buy their avatars extra lives for just $1.99 (with down-the-line charges strategically hidden). Silicon Valley must be run by a star chamber of soulless profiteers, right? Where is their collective sense of responsibility?

This sentiment is neither fair nor realistic. Companies exist to create and sell products people want to use. To do so, they must engage with customers in the most effective ways possible—hopefully delighting rather than alienating them.

And in case you still want to blame Mark Zuckerberg for making Facebook so irresistible, consider another conclusion from the aforementioned study. Unlike the brains of cocaine addicts, the part of the brain that inhibits compulsive Facebook use works just fine. You can choose to cut back on the social media crack; you just don't want to.[8] As much as studies on the brain can give us powerful clues into the way we work, the reality is we love to be victims. It's much easier—and satisfying—to blame someone else instead of ourselves. Whether it's the latest report on TechCrunch or an interview with Tristan Harris on "60 Minutes" telling us we're being programmed,[9] if we can find something that reinforces our behavior as out of our control, we'll take it. After all, it's so much more fun to scroll endlessly on Facebook than finish that project we know we should be doing.

In other words, we can control such behavior but don't. After all, it's not illegal and doesn't seem obviously harmful. (More important, why hasn't anyone liked my vacation pictures yet?)

The problem is that we cede this control throughout the day and don't correctly value the time we lose.

Social reciprocity is a prime example. If someone mentions us on LinkedIn or Facebook, a notification kindly pops up on our screen. Maybe someone liked our comment. Or hated our post (and felt it was her civic duty to tell us in the comments section).

Once the suspense is over, we find ourselves in the wilderness of a bottomless feed. Twenty minutes disappear as we chase intriguing distractions.

In the same way, it feels rude not to answer a text. And when the boss e-mails a question, we're expected to reply, often immediately.

As leaders, we often set up these systems without focus in mind, inadvertently creating open avenues for distraction.

Focus-wise technology is essential to the constantly connected workplace. It encourages the smartest allocation of your people's attention, promoting focus and effective management.

And it starts with a simple but profound question: *Are you serving technology or is technology serving you?*

There is a way to enjoy the efficiency our technology provides without becoming the tools of our tools. In other words, don't be a tool. It's time to realize we control technology, not the other way around.

For our technology to serve us, and not the other way around, we can use these three guiding principles:

1. Does it promote or prevent focus?

2. Does it save or sap attention resources?

3. Does it encourage or erode engagement?

CHAPTER 11

Message Undeliverable

G reat strategies for technology use are all about the effective creation and removal of access to technology and each other.

The number one question to ask about technology for your organization is: Does it promote or prevent focus?

Let's look at what focus-wise technology provides to help us preserve attention.

BARRIERS TO ACCESS

Access is good—and addicting. The key is to control it.

Not by branding time on social media as theft or logging bathroom breaks to discourage phone use, something my client sorely regretted. (We'll discuss the wrong ways to control access in Chapter 13.)

Technology purveyors used to be so fixated on access that they paid scant attention to barriers. Programs either didn't offer any, or they made users hunt for them. (How many of your employees know about Do Not Disturb mode on the iPhone?)

Focus-wise technology grants us control—which we then have to control.

The first step in exercising this control is surprisingly simple yet shockingly ignored by most people: Understand the capabilities of the tech we already own and put them to use.

A friend recently demanded a group WhatsApp thread stop sending texts between 11 PM and 7 AM as a claim of common sense manners. Although everyone respected his wish to be off the grid, they didn't respect the way he approached it. The group responded by doubling down on after-hours texts. The reason was simple: WhatsApp offers the ability to mute conversations and turn off push. Asking others to change their behavior to suit you when the tech now grants you control is unrealistic and lazy.

Gmail has a pause feature. IM programs feature "snooze" or "away" settings. And then there's always the good old "out of office" option, which may be an employee's best digital friend. Rather than complain about 24/7 access, use these features.

I'm not suggesting a sensory deprivation tank. It's about asking employees to turn off access for, say, 45 minutes while they focus on a specific project.

Below are two simple but effective mobile-device modes.

Do Not Disturb

A great feature when you can't turn off your phone. It lets you choose which calls and texts come through (maybe the boss or an employee who needs to reach you). On the iPhone, you can restrict access to your Favorites list. Android phones let you tailor access with rules that automatically turn off ringers, alarms, and alerts for events or specific blocks of time.

Airplane

For everyone from millennials to baby boomers, shutting off the phone can be borderline traumatic. Airplane mode (no cell service or Wi-Fi) preserves the comforts of camera, clock, and downloaded music while otherwise blocking out the world. A simple toggle opens the door to true focus and productivity.

Of course, it's one thing to turn off access, quite another to *keep* it turned off. All those marshmallows—calls, texts, Instagram alerts— are just waiting to tumble down on us. That's why we need to equip our teams with tools that eliminate the temptation during focused work time.

The idea is to make the pain of access exceed the reward of access. If you have to climb a rope (one that will tear up your hands) to get the marshmallow, you might just eat the broccoli and call it a day. Lockout tools can be your rope. They are programs and apps that block users during a given period or make reconnection difficult. Here are the categories I recommend:

- Internet blocking. These literally turn off access for however long you set them. Getting back online can mean a full reboot, squarely emphasizing pain over reward. There are also versions of this that can limit your Web access to specific sites you are actively using at the moment (i.e., a cloud-based accounting program might require you to be online, but you don't want to be able to check the stock ticker until after you are done).

- Gamification. These apps make a game out of staying off your phone and other devices.

- Simplified word processing. One example is iA Writer, a straightforward program that eliminates all the distracting bells and whistles. Another one that I like is called Bear, which can double as a note-taking system.

- E-mail cleanup. Programs that, for instance, unsubscribe you from e-mails while grouping others into a single daily digest to minimize interruption throughout the day.

LIMITS TO EXCESSIVE SWITCHING

Most of us have a minimum of three programs open at a given time: a Web browser, an e-mail program, and whatever tool is devoted to our focused work. Our friend, Harry, ups the ante with 15 open tabs on his browser, including IM, Spotify, and his Facebook and Instagram feeds.

Just as he starts to roll on a project, an e-mail fades into view, demanding to be opened. It's another useless comment on a useless string, but he answers it anyway. An IM flashes. A colleague asks the same question Harry has already answered by e-mail and text. He patiently answers again.

Then his Spotify jolts him with…accordion classics? Have to remedy that.

Part of Harry's frustration is that he doesn't really understand the source of it. It's all just a normal day at work for him.

Flipping between programs breeds distraction. Our minds have to shift gears to focus on a new source (as we learned in Chapter 4), not to mention the distraction that comes from the program we're switching to.

Good technology—and focus-wise use of it—helps us reduce the switch count. Reducing the number of open programs and windows is an obvious place to start. As mentioned, Do Not Disturb and Airplane modes help as well (browser tabs can be cached before Wi-Fi is turned off).

But though these are important habits to cultivate, they rest largely with your employees. A more institutional problem is collaboration and workflow.

Technology, historically, has separated work from where we communicate and team up about it. E-mail, therefore, becomes the default for talking to each other about a project, constantly forcing us to switch away from the work itself. Focus and productivity invariably suffer.

Document collaboration systems such as Google Docs solve this problem by creating a single place to do everything, from adding questions and comments to tracking updates. Everyone can focus on a shared doc instead of switching programs to work on or discuss it.

When a program doesn't naturally facilitate communication, project-management software can unify platforms for a specific workflow (more on this in Section 5). You might, for example, combine product design with an initiative such as overseas expansion.

Companies are taking notice. Global sales of collaborative software are projected to reach $20.1 billion in 2020, compared with $13.3 billion in 2015, according to research cited in CIO Insight.[1] But a survey also reveals that professionals want systems to be easier to set up and use while allowing access for contractors, consultants, and other partners.[2] Which leads us to the next category.

UTILITY AND SIMPLE DESIGN

Microsoft Word does the job and then some—a *lot* more "some." It wouldn't surprise me if Word could walk my dog and rock my son to sleep.

But how many of us use all those icons and commands when writing a document? Fonts, layout options, WordArt—it's easy for the project itself to become the distraction as formatting takes center stage. And then there are the times formatting becomes the distraction itself. Nothing is more infuriating—and time-wasting—than Word deciding you wanted a new outline format instead of continuing what you've been using for the last 15 lines!

Just because technology can offer a feature doesn't always mean it should. Less truly can be more.

Gabe Cooper, an award-winning software designer who has collaborated with my company, lives by this maxim. As founder of Brushfire Interactive and Virtuous Software, he helps some of the world's biggest companies choose programs with simple design and function.

Cooper cites two of the most common mistakes in tech design.

The Kitchen Sink App

Nervous organizations, especially larger ones, pile on 74 features instead of honing in on one that can be communicated in 15 seconds. *We gotta hit everything!* When users describe the app to someone else, they end up saying, "It does this . . . and this . . . and this . . ."

This is a problem of focus. An app should fit in an elevator pitch.

Similarly, we often seek to find the tech equivalent of Gollum's precious from *The Lord of the Rings*—one tech to rule them all. We want a single program to integrate and fulfill all of our needs. And tech companies claim they can do just that. Project management, messaging, task lists, client relationship management, calendars—they all seem to do it all. That doesn't mean they do them all well. It's more helpful to think about the wide variety of functions they actually serve. The modern-day equivalent of your Rolodex, calendar, fax machine, pen and paper, chalkboard, and administrative assistant needn't be provided by a single company. Pick the application for what it does best. If you need the applications to integrate, third-party software such as IFTTT can fill the gaps.

Too Much of a Bad Thing

People won't share ugliness with others (unless they're ridiculing it). And if ugliness had a recipe, clutter would be the main ingredient. That's what happens when you pack too much into design and functionality.

Users "may say they want more functionality and more buttons, but they don't," Cooper says. "They want one button that's super simple, that's elegant and gorgeous.... And that's way more exaggerated on mobile than it is on the Web."

Easy to look at and easy to use—the recipe for tech success.

In this chapter, we asked a simple but profound question: Does the technology you use promote or prevent focus? Focus-wise technology provides barriers to access, discourages excessive switching between programs, and favors utility and simple design. That leads to focus and ultimately freedom—the subject of our next chapter.

CHAPTER 12

Free at Last

The second key question to becoming focus-wise in your use of technology is: Does your technology sap or save attention resources?

Freedom to focus thrives with the efficient capturing and sharing of information, elimination of errors, and ease of use. It ultimately increases both productivity and innovation.

Until now in this book, innovation has taken a backseat to understanding the causes and costs of distraction in the constantly connected workplace. It's time to remember the big picture. What is your goal?

The key initiatives that drive business, whether they be innovation, process improvement, project execution, or simple selling, all thrive when our teams are focused on the most important things. Consider Harry and Jack. On Monday afternoon, they both had a moment of insight about how to improve their businesses. This epiphany is like the beginning embers of a new fire. If it is nourished, it can expand into a raging inferno. If neglected, it will be snuffed out, as though it never happened.

In Harry's excitement, he vets his idea with his peers. They're excited. He's excited. Before long, though, Harry's routine catches up with him. His wife sends him a few texts about their weekend plans, and as he plans his weekend, his work-related e-mails back up. Worse, many of those e-mails don't require him to think. He simply has to perform the rote exercises.

Harry looks up a document to e-mail to Susie in accounting. He opens the spreadsheet he's been authoring to copy and paste today's business data into an e-mail for Tim's big meeting tomorrow.

He has a couple of generic e-mails to respond to from his team. By the time Harry is caught up, Monday is over, and there are already a few things to do Tuesday morning. His moment of inspiration has been relegated to the "pipe dream" part of his brain, forgotten for now, only to be revisited when he's uniquely dissatisfied with the status quo. The world dictates Harry's priorities at any given moment—and those interruptions kill his innovative thinking.

Jack, on the other hand, immediately recognizes the value of his idea. Rather than interrupting his work to shop the idea, Jack does something he does with many of his thoughts: He uses technology to prioritize it for further consideration. He knows his inspirations need time and space to develop and that time and space isn't available right now.

Before Jack begins his commute home Monday, he opens the Evernote list he uses to track his work thoughts. Jack reads his description of the idea and begins to focus. By the time he's arrived home, Jack understands the problem he's solving and how to document it. Jack knows the value of his solution and how it will improve the business. Jack knows which coworkers need to be involved to initiate the change. Lastly, Jack knows where this fits on the list of important tasks demanding his time and whether it is an immediate priority. Tomorrow, Jack will bring his idea to life. And that's why he's a high-impact contributor.

Your people can be too. Let's examine what our tools must do to help free up focus.

CAPTURE AND SHARE

An e-mail contains data that will seal a presentation, potentially securing millions in new business. If only you could find it.

A search (was the metric page views, clicks, or conversion?) highlights hundreds of e-mails but not the one you need. Wait! You're in the wrong folder. Has to be this one . . . nope, still nothing.

Maybe if you could remember when it was sent and who sent it. You narrow down dates and possible senders. You even poke your head into the hall and ask out loud.

You can retrieve troves of data you need from one system, but it isn't formatted for what you need.

You sent a request for feedback on a report to 15 peers a week ago. Naturally, it wasn't urgent then, so today you're getting flooded with 15 edited versions of a document with week-old data.

Over and over again, my clients complain that the very technology designed to make them more efficient actually stymies them. I've seen companies deploy systems that made employees feel like they were spending the day reporting about work instead of actually doing it. It doesn't help when "solutions" commonly include 20-year-old database technology while MS Office (Word released in 1987, Excel in 1985) serves as the bridge for the inevitable process gaps.

As a leader, you need to determine whether your technology for creating, storing, retrieving, and consuming information preserves or squanders employees' attention. A focused work environment has tools to manage both enterprise and personal information. To better navigate this complexity, ask yourself the following questions.

What Type of Information Will It Manage?

Attention isn't purely a technology problem. Remember Jack? He used Evernote to bookmark an idea for later consideration. The simple utility of a tool at his fingertips to capture and organize his ideas allowed Jack to focus where he was needed. It enabled him to reflect deeply on his idea when he was free to focus without distraction. Evernote is a private, always-on utility with the flexibility to capture any type of thought, idea, or inspiration.

Conversely, most business tools need to be collaborative. It's rarely enough to have the idea or the information; you have to be able to communicate it, support it with data, include others in your thought process, and easily make adjustments.

Keep in mind attention is a problem that happens at the intersection of man and machine; if your tools require a lot of manual management to accomplish simple collaboration, you're inviting distraction into your office.

Is Information Easy to Capture?

Today's worker doesn't know where to put her ideas. A yellow pad sits on her desk for note-taking, but how can she share an idea without having to reproduce it in a different format? What if she loses the pad or spills her latté on it?

Your people can do way better than yellow-lined paper. Smart-phone software, for example, can capture, store, and back up notes for easy access.

Choosing the right tool can feel daunting; every day seems to bring a new app promising to solve your productivity challenges. Ironically, the focus needed to learn and use these tools can sap our attention—the very resource they were meant to save.

That's why I limit my suggestions to just a few organizational products, including Evernote and Asana (also Bear if you have an Apple device). Whatever program you use, each makes the information you store more useful.

Evernote, my go-to, is all about "notebooks," and how you use them makes all the difference. My two basic notebook types are "capture" and "recall." For the first type, I have three categories:

Active. My first "main" notebook contains anything I'm working on. Whenever I have an idea but don't want to think about filing, it goes here.

A-Thoughts. A repository of random thoughts and ideas in a given month. Cool quotes, process improvements, diet suggestions to explore later—they all go in this notebook. (I call it "A-Thoughts" because Evernote organizes notebooks in alphabetical order.)

Articles not yet read. I want to read them but not just yet.

Is Information Easy to Organize and Recall?

Captured information isn't of much use if you can't access it easily. That brings me to the "recall" notebook mentioned above.

Eventually, ideas and thoughts from my capture notebooks are organized into their own recall subcategories, such as motivations and quotes, product improvement, business units, life hacks, and family and parenting. The simpler, the better.

Some material gets filed immediately if the category is obvious. But often I'll just put thoughts and ideas in my recall folders for later review. (The bottom line for any organizational system: You and your people won't use it if it demands that ideas be stored right away.)

The key to my success with this method has been scheduling *thought review* times every two months (once a month proved too unrealistic). This way, I read my thoughts at least once more than I otherwise would have. You may find it helpful to actually schedule these sessions on your calendar. Ideas go to their best corresponding category; the best are then copied into next month's notes for even further review.

Another crucial feature saves both time and attention: content preview. Instead of physically opening and closing files, you can often get what you need at a glance. We may be talking an extra minute or so. But that can mean the difference between frustration and functionality.

Just the sort of low barrier the Harrys of the world need for capturing and nurturing ideas.

AUTOMATE, AUTOMATE, AUTOMATE

There's a great debate in business around automation right now. There are some who believe it is the single greatest threat to the American worker and others who believe it's the dawn of a new age of opportunity.

Chad Sparber is the chair of economics at Colgate University, and he says it like this: "Technological developments have increasingly replaced low- and mid-skilled jobs while complementing higher-skilled jobs."[1]

Focus on the implications of that statement for a moment. It implies the automation you're looking for isn't the tool that will eliminate your workforce but rather the tool that will eliminate the lowest value work for your workforce. The good news is there are businesses already built on their ability to do just this.

There's a technology company named Workiva, based in the sleepy college town of Ames, Iowa. If you've never heard of them, I'm not surprised. They had zero customers in 2009. Yet by 2016, Workiva's Enterprise platform had become the industry standard in financial reporting and was being used by more than 70 percent of Fortune 500 businesses.

Their perspective was simple: The biggest hurdle to productivity in business was not the people in the process but instead the tools they had at their disposal.

Entire processes had been built around Word, Excel, Power-Point, and Outlook, and the distraction cost of jumping from e-mail to spreadsheet to document and back was profoundly expensive.

Workiva built a customer base by empowering workers with a force multiplier. In their platform, a single data change can be applied to every relevant document, spreadsheet, calculation, graph, and presentation. Workiva built a cloud-based infrastructure that virtually eliminates copy-paste and repeat reporting siloes, driving real-time collaboration.

Bel Fuse Inc., a manufacturer of electronic-circuit products, used to send a team of four to each office for internal audits and review. The company added locations after two large acquisitions, nearly doubling sales and tripling the workload. Clearly the old way of working would no longer work.

Bel Fuse responded by buying Workiva Wdesk, a cloud-based productivity platform that centralizes sharing, reporting, and analysis. Teams anywhere in the world could collaborate simultaneously on a document (word processing, spreadsheet, or presentation) with a full audit trail of changes.

Platforms like Wdesk do much of the tedious and heavy work (such as data crunching), reducing workload and freeing employees to focus on what they do best.

The idea of automation is at once revered and reviled. It certainly costs jobs and will continue to do so. But in the twenty-first century, we simply can't deny our people the tools that free them from exasperating work.

Why did Charlene, our expense-report maven from Section 2, want to quit? Because her job asked her to be a robot instead of letting her do what robots can't: apply creativity and problem-solving to a task.

Focus-wise technology reduces errors while increasing efficiency. It empowers employees to do what they truly care about and think big. Ultimately, that means less stress and more happiness.

BE EASY TO USE

Companies often fall in love with the most expensive technology available only to find that employees ignore it. "Too tough to use," they might say, or "I like the old platform."

The problem with most technology that fails to get adopted is that it requires user expertise. If the user must be an expert, adoption is a challenge.

People want to feel comfortable with their tools. New tech that mimics tech they're used to is adopted more readily. When an inefficient system is what they're used to (probably why it's being replaced), good training fills the gap (which we discuss in Chapter 22). A low learning curve combined with high user-friendliness is the ticket.

Take, for instance, Hackensack Meridian Health Pascack Valley Medical Center in New Jersey. They aim to provide patients with both the most comfortable experience possible and top-notch clinical care. However, they faced a challenge in balancing nursing time to accommodate both of these patient needs. The nurses were spending more than half their time providing nonclinical "comfort care" to patients rather than the clinical care they've been expertly trained to deliver.

Patients regularly turned to the nurse call button for all of their needs—from help with their in-room TV and phone to meal ordering, clergy requests, and housekeeping needs. Nurses became the middlemen, processing requests for other departments to work on the issue. The end result was a costly, inefficient game of telephone tag that delayed service delivery to patients and unnecessarily tied up clinically trained, skilled nurses and reduced their job satisfaction.

Knowing that employees will forsake time savings and even career advancement when technology confounds them or doesn't serve them well, the administrators at Pascack Valley made identifying a solution that worked for everyone a priority, and they found it with GoMo Health Bedside Concierge.

This solution allowed patients to submit their "in-the-moment" requests directly to the appropriate department for fulfillment via mobile. The simple-to-use, no-app-to-download, cloud-based program is available 24/7, enhancing the patient experience and simplifying the overall service delivery. By focusing on painting the picture of how this technology could impact the quality of time spent on direct patient care, Pascack Valley saw swift adoption of the technology and an eagerness from the nursing team to introduce it to patients.

And, importantly, it was simple for the patients to use. The nurses stopped being the middlemen, requests were filled faster, patients were happier, and nurses' joy in practice increased.

In the process, Pascack estimated they recaptured nearly 59 hours per month in nursing time, an annual savings of more than $28,000— all from one small but important, easy-to-use, and affordable technology solution.

By putting these focus-wise principles around technology into action, you and your organization can move from being a tool of your tool to leveraging it for greater productivity and profitability. All it takes is a simple mindset shift. Next, we'll look at how technology can give you just the right level of visibility into your employees' work.

CHAPTER 13

Best Buddy or Big Brother?

The final question to ask to become focus-wise in your use of technology is: Does your technology encourage or erode engagement?

If focused attention is a commodity, then focus-wise technology can help determine how your organization's attention resources are being spent. It's neither realistic nor desirable for employees to focus on work 100 percent of the time. We all need the relief of a cat video (or its equivalent) once in a while.

But what if your employees wasted hours every week watching and sharing a feline-palooza of videos?

Today's technology can virtually tell you anything you want to know about employee behavior. Anything. The question is no longer what can you know? It's what should you know to get the best performance at the lowest attention and financial cost? And that is not a simple question.

A rising number of companies are using productivity-monitoring software to watch employees and see exactly how they spend their time. The roughly $200 million monitoring industry is expected to grow to $500 million by 2020.[1]

George Orwell might nod at this.

But is it really Big Brother? Or just a concerned friend looking out for everyone's well-being?

People tend to work better when they're being watched. It's called the Hawthorne effect: Those being studied change their behavior simply *because* they're being studied.

A friend who used to work construction told me that everyone goofed off when the boss left. When the boss returned, the pace picked up. Workers didn't feel like they were being babysat; they just instinctively worked harder to look good for management.

Would employee focus improve if we could monitor how they're feeling? Bank of America is among the companies that have explored systems "that monitor worker emotions to boost performance and compliance," *MIT Sloan Management Review* reports.[2]

On the other hand, employees who feel mistrusted or mistreated also feel less engaged. It's hard to imagine a resulting increase in productivity—the reason for monitoring in the first place.

So is monitoring our people even worth it?

There's research behind both views.

MY BUDDY AND ME

It's never been easier for organizations to analyze their employees and see how they spend their time. A hospital near Orlando, Florida, used monitoring software to track nurses and care staff during their shifts.[3] Employees wore badges embedded with sensors, allowing administrators to pinpoint visits to patients, the nurses' station, and supply rooms.

The software uncovered inefficiencies—such as when certain supply rooms were understocked, forcing nurses to walk farther for what they needed. The problem was fixed, and the staff was grateful.

We don't tend to think of this as Big Brother. It's more like Helpful Buddy who heeds the Google mantra of "don't be evil." Any forfeiture of privacy is mitigated by the beneficial use of gathered information.

In the same vein, software can now monitor every keystroke and website visit—accountability that improves productivity. It's Hawthorne in action: Once employees know they're being watched, they become more efficient.

Such technology also reveals speedbumps and waste. Are employees losing time switching between tasks? Do their programs create distraction? Armed with answers, employers can address issues and train their staff to be more efficient.

And monitoring is fast becoming indispensable for organizations with teams at multiple locations. As I remind clients, you can no longer manage people by just walking around the office. Many employees work on different continents.

Telling patterns and variables also emerge from tracking. A FedEx driver I know swears by the company's monitoring policies. FedEx knows the location of every driver at a given moment, routes taken, and time spent at each stop.

The data leads to more efficient routes, allowing him to finish shifts more quickly. He just goes where his GPS tells him. "Sometimes I have no idea why they send me the way they do," he says. "But they know the quickest way."

Finally, monitoring can also improve employee training. "This call might be monitored for quality assurance purposes" goes way beyond what we could have imagined just a few years ago.

Some call-center employers now receive real-time coaching from artificial intelligence software that evaluates their speech and interactions. I did a six-city tour with one of these companies to speak to their clients alongside a demonstration of their newest product. It was amazing what they equip their people with to shape the customer experience.[4] Their AI adviser might suggest talking more slowly or warn them that the customer appears upset.

Helpful Buddy, at your service.

Big Brother Is Watching

Employees unhappy with being watched often aren't concerned about privacy. What irks them is the result of the watching: bad decisions that diminish their work lives.

A company that blocks social media during work hours might also be blocking key sources of creativity. Many graphic designers, for example, frequent Pinterest for inspiration. Blocking it actually *stunts* their productivity.

And when organizations restrict their computers, the action doesn't necessarily apply to personal phones. Employees simply switch to their own devices for full Internet access.

This echoes back to the futility of "social media as theft." In a Cisco survey of 3,600 younger workers, 56 percent said they would ignore a workplace ban on social media or not accept the job in the first place.[5]

Late-night talk show host Jimmy Fallon summed up the issue: "A college in Pennsylvania is blocking computer access to social-networking sites for an entire week and then requiring the students to write an essay about the experience. Yep. The essay will be called, 'We All Have Smartphones, Dumb-Ass.'"[6]

It becomes much less funny when we veer into privacy concerns. In *The Circle*, a novel by Dave Eggers, a powerful tech company develops real-time cameras that users wear to become "transparent," sharing every detail of their lives. Privacy isn't just lost; it becomes, in a perversion of Google's philosophy, the evil that society needs to oppose. Of course, this isn't just the stuff of fiction. Companies like Buffer actually use the word "transparent" in glowing fashion, patting themselves on the back for opening up everyone's e-mail to the whole company for reading.[7] Of course, the dark underbelly of this transparency is that people find workarounds. If e-mail is open, they'll text instead.

Or even more extreme, consider Epicenter, a company in Sweden where employees enthusiastically volunteer to be chipped.[8]

Implanted between thumb and forefinger, the rice grain-sized microchip lets workers open doors, use printers, and buy food with a wave of their hand. Epicenter employees love the convenience and future-cool of being "cyborgs."

They seem to give less thought to the employee data that's being generated, information that could ultimately subvert their privacy and leave them vulnerable to hackers.

A final strike at Big Brother is the Pygmalion effect: the tendency for people to act the way they're treated. Employees treated with suspicion are more likely to fulfill the perception.

Is there a way to see how our people allocate attention without alienating them?

FINDING BALANCE IN TECHNOLOGY

The idea of Big Brother is a great placeholder for trepidation about technology at work and in the larger world. The truth is you can harness tech to the benefit of everyone in your organization. Following are a few things to consider when debating how to use tech for visibility insights at your company.

Individual Accountability

The information harvested in *The Circle*, and even in the real-life example of Epicenter, is itself neither good nor bad. The question is how it's used and who benefits from it.

People will trade privacy for convenience and insight (which may explain the parties Epicenter employees throw for colleagues agreeing to be chipped). Insight can lead to accountability, then self-improvement. On the other hand, they will riot over privacy concerns when they perceive the technology is giving them neither.

Last year, a friend of mine joined Weight Watchers, downloaded the app, and set his goals. Traditionally, members went to meetings to hold themselves accountable.

But my friend never attended a meeting. He simply entered everything he ate and detailed each minute of exercise. The app tracked his daily points and showed his progress throughout the day.

At first, his daily points ran out sooner than expected. Weight Watchers has a saying: "If you bite it, you write it." So in went the muffins, M&Ms, and cookie dough (and all happiness, I would imagine).

The picture that emerged motivated him to improve his diet and fitness. The app transformed select bits of his private life into usable insights.

As leaders, we can take a valuable lesson from a simple diet app. Sometimes our people don't realize how much time they're wasting. We can provide technology that lets them see exactly what they're doing so they can boost productivity on their own.

Rather than using the tool to punish those who spend too much time browsing social media, use it to reward those who are particularly disciplined. This subtle choice is the difference between employees viewing leadership as members of their team and an us-versus-them culture. No one works hard to help the other team succeed.

Analyzing "Safe" Data

With the right guardrails, you can use technology to get unprecedented visibility into what is happening in your organization.

A client of mine with hundreds of remote teams around the world wanted to find out how much time employees spent on e-mail. Were there particular teams that were more distracted? Any who managed communication flow distinctly well? While they have full access to all emails sent through their server, they rightfully considered the relational and time cost of mining through all employee e-mails. PKC Security, a boutique tech consultancy the client had used in the past, offered a unique solution. Since the cybersecurity company had experience with surveillance, they used tools to protect employee privacy while extracting useful data. They created a product that analyzed the metadata like subject lines, dates, senders, and recipients without reviewing actual e-mail content.

It's amazing what you can learn from "safe" data—information that no one cares you know. From a month of email records, PKC identified which tasks employees wasted the most time on, which teams collaborated well, which were micromanaged (or passive aggressive), which employees were distracted or distracting others, and which teams most likely would ditch email for tools like Slack.

This is the actual graphic they created (Figure 13.1). When visualizing how teams send e-mails, the teams that communicated most efficiently looked like large interconnected blobs, with members e-mailing one another directly. Less functional teams looked like a hub and spoke: The person in the middle was the one most likely to slow everyone down, distracted by managing e-mails that kept the whole team coordinated. The total number of e-mails as well as the ratio of interconnected blobs to hub and spokes patterns speaks to the overall health of how the organization communicates.

The visual representation of the data gave leaders the insights they needed to help teams, adjust processes, select technology, and develop

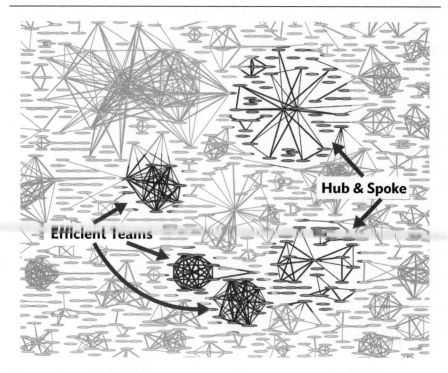

Figure 13.1 Visual Representation of E-mail Communication in a Global Organization over One Month.

targeted communication skills training; all while protecting the privacy and trust of the employees.

Forming Habits

In the same way we use technology for individual accountability, we can promote tools that help our people self-manage and create good habits.

Routine is a foundation of quality focus. And it doesn't actually take long to replace bad habits with good ones. Once rewired, our brains can help us cut through distractions more easily.

Infusionsoft, which makes customer relationship management and marketing automation software for small businesses, uses a reporting tool called Execute To Win to enhance self-management and good habit-building. ETW helps employees establish and track their goals, providing visibility to managers.

At Infusionsoft, employees give weekly updates on their top three quarterly goals. They can label a goal's status—"on track" or "falling behind," for example—allowing the company to make adjustments and get ahead of problems.

In writing this book, I've been using Streaks, a simple app that lets me set daily tasks with the goal of turning them into habits. Streaks accommodates as many as six activities, anything from flossing to walking the dog. Every time I complete a task, my streak is extended—a great way to rewire the brain for productivity.

One Platform

We discussed how moving communication to the platform you are working from can reduce switching and thus increase focus. There's another benefit in the category of visibility. Efficiency and transparency increase if you can keep work and communication on a single platform that integrates well with other tech.

With project-management programs such as Basecamp, Asana, and Trello, you can create tasks, check in, and course-adjust for changing conditions. (Asana, in fact, is helping expedite this book by keeping me in sync with my editors at every stage of production.)

These tools facilitate workflow by consolidating all conversations and content germane to a project without forcing your people to switch between programs. Projects are moved in stages for full visibility. The programs also play well with e-mail and content management systems, for instance, so that no details fall through the cracks.

Technology that's focus-wise serves you and your people instead of the other way around.

Now That I Have Your Attention . . .

For Section 4 reflection questions, summary video, and next step resources, please visit focuswise.com/book

SECTION FIVE

FOCUS-WISE COMMUNICATION

CHAPTER 14

Can You Hear Me Now?

In 2002, one of my clients sent an e-mail to his 10,000 subscribers letting them know about a book he had just written.

He sold 1,000 copies the first week in direct response to the e-mail and another 1,000 over the next month.

A 20 percent response. Not too shabby.

Fast-forward to the present. His platform has exploded. He has written countless books (some of them best-sellers in their Amazon category), is regularly interviewed on radio and TV, and has more speaking requests than he can handle.

He sent an e-mail to his expanded list promoting his newest book. After tweeting about it, he posted on three other social media platforms. He was retweeted by several people who have more than 100,000 followers.

He received less than a 1 percent response. His message got lost in the noise.

In 2002, people eagerly opened their inboxes to see what was waiting for them. Back then, every store wasn't asking for your e-mail when you bought a pair of shoes or a blender. Bills weren't in your inbox. E-mail wasn't in your pocket.

In 2002, my client's readers saw his e-mail and opened it with enthusiasm. Today, they love him even more.

But they just can't hear him.

LOST IN THE NOISE

Communication has always been difficult. As the psychologist and philosopher Williams James said, "The greatest gap that exists in the universe is that between one human mind and another."

The digital age promised to narrow this gap but increased it instead. We can reach each other anytime in an almost infinite number of ways. But every place you turn is already filled with noise by the time you get there. (Justin Bieber launched his career on YouTube in 2008.) Good luck finding the *next* Bieber amid the gazillion videos aspiring singers have posted since then.)

Whatever you say in today's noisy marketplace isn't likely to be heard. And if it is, it probably won't be remembered. You bring your golden ticket to Willie Wonka's chocolate factory and find yourself among millions of other people waving tickets. (And Augustus has already contaminated the chocolate river!)

Reaching your audience is no longer the challenge; it's knowing how to speak over everyone else so that you're heard, again and again. Attention, as we recall from Chapter 2, is our most valuable currency. And its value continues to soar.

Reach is a two-way street. The world is relentlessly vying for the attention of you and your people, an ant trail of technology curling its way into the office. As leaders, we need to mitigate entry, creating an environment that helps our people focus on the right things at the right time.

Living in a digital world has changed the communication game in more and wider ways than you know, making it both easier and harder.

Buried under E-mail

The volume of e-mail has never been higher, and it's still growing. By the end of 2021, the total number of business and consumer e-mails will reach nearly 320 billion per day, according to The Radicati Group.[1] That's a colossal increase over the 269 billion we already send and receive today.

Even though social media itself has soared, most platforms still require an e-mail address to sign up. It's the same with banking and shopping. E-mail may have long lost its cool factor, but we can't quit it:

- The average office worker receives 121 e-mails a day
- More than 49 percent of those e-mails are spam
- Two percent have a malicious attachment
- Fifty-five percent are opened on a desktop
- Twenty-five percent are opened on a smartphone
- E-mails most likely to be opened are sent on a Saturday
- E-mails least likely to be opened are sent on a Friday[2]
- Forty-two percent of Americans check their e-mail in the bathroom
- Eighteen percent of Americans check their e-mail while driving.[3] (Arrrgh! Pay attention to the road, people.)

E-mail frequently fails as communication because people equate *responsiveness* with *responsibility*. E-mail trumps any other task we should be doing, so we suffer through all of it—the relevant and the inconsequential—to make sure the one e-mail we need doesn't get lost in the noise. This signal-to-noise ratio dooms e-mail to inefficiency.

Yet, though everyone complains about their inboxes, nobody is sending fewer messages. E-mail has proven to be a staple of our digital diets, one that doesn't require an actual conversation or any other heavy social lifting. You can just shoot out a quick note and switch to the next new message. (Hello, dopamine.)

As for instant messaging, it's second verse, same as the first. And the sheer number of messages we send and receive merrily increases.

We like sending and receiving. The noise is comforting. It makes us feel social, busy, and even important. There's evidence that merely anticipating the possibility of a message releases dopamine; it's also released when we anticipate sending a message.

But that cascade of messages threatens to paralyze us. It creates an overload of options, which can push us into decisions against our own interest.[4] At work, this can mean a lack of organization that hurts performance. When an employee feels bombarded, he is more likely to retreat to the relative sanctuary of Instagram or Facebook.

Someone Call a Meeting

With the seemingly endless forms of communication that the digital world offers us, you might assume fewer meetings would be a benefit. You would assume poorly. The constantly connected world laughs at our optimistic intent. More access creates more meetings than ever and stunts our productivity.

And the meetings themselves are impacted as task-switching participants give only a fraction—or any—of their focus. Which makes sense. If you have a ton of meetings, then you need to get your other work done sometime. But this ironically leads to more meetings because no one paid attention in the first one.

And much like e-mail, we love the "benefits" that meetings provide us. It's a lot of fun to do an internal road show and walk your colleagues through that PowerPoint you painstakingly put together. We also love the access that meetings give us to people and their brain share. In a world where our focus is so fractured, there is a constant, nagging feeling that maybe our solutions and work aren't as good as they could be. Tapping into the insights and ideas of others can alleviate that fear—and displace blame should things go wrong. Of course, this slows work down immensely and can water down good and courageous ideas.

Technology allows us to schedule more meetings. So we do. And people can attend without being physically present (or psychically present, if they're on vacation). Meeting creep has advanced to the point that we spend more time talking about our work than doing it. "I have to finish this major proposal. How about, rather than doing that, I call a meeting to talk with others about ways we can improve the proposal that I'm avoiding?"

In the same way that e-mail overload can paralyze us, excessive meetings are a response to feeling overwhelmed—a result of poor attention allocation—as opposed to being genuinely overworked. Meetings become a way to look busy in lieu of actually focusing on the work—or a futile attempt to *find* focus in the work.

One company spent a mind-blowing 300,000 employee hours a year on a single weekly executive committee meeting (for context, each of us gets only about 8,700 hours a year total, including sleep).[5] And research from Bain & Company revealed that a typical manager loses 16 hours a week herding e-mails and going to unnecessary meetings.[6]

The Relic of Hierarchy

Historically, organizations have structured communication through a natural hierarchy that mimics the military. Decisions flow from the top down through the ranks. Concerns and suggestions come from any level and go to the direct report.

Many older leaders still operate from this model, and it drives younger employees crazy.

It's not because younger employees are a bunch of narcissists who want to be best buddies with the CEO (even if true, that's not the problem). It's because the through-the-ranks method of communication is predicated on *communication access* as the bottleneck. And that's no longer the case.

In a world with direct access to everyone (including our celebrity crush on Twitter), these employees assume they should communicate directly with whoever would most benefit from the information: "Forget my manager. I want to text Jeff Bezos."

Now it's the seven layers of leadership between employee and CEO who are being driven crazy.

The question isn't who is right and who is wrong. It's how do we get people with radically different life experiences and expectations on the same page.

The Communication Compact

As leaders, we must steer communication to the right channels so that everyone feels heard and valued. And because we communicate about everything *except* how we communicate, I recommend one in-person meeting per year where you communicate about *how* you interact in all facets—from texts to e-mails to meetings to lines of communication. The results of this meeting are what we call a Communication Compact with your team.

A Communication Compact is one of the most valuable tools we offer to clients at Focuswise. It's a social contract that outlines expectations and consequences of communication within your team.

In this annual team meeting, discuss the challenges and expectations. We have a guide we use (available at focuswise.com/cihya/five), but you can start even simpler by asking employees a simple question: What are your three biggest communication challenges? Afterward, implement what you learned. Collaborate on how to handle these issues while also addressing channel selections and response times and reducing volume.

It's critical to *not* unilaterally dictate the rules that govern your team. By making it a group process, you ensure buy-in. And don't worry; you aren't the only one annoyed by Jim's consistent tendency to CC everyone and Jane's really annoying phone-during-the-entire-meeting habit (probably checking Instagram). Trust the group, and you will get the benefits you're looking for. Plus, employees want to be heard—a lot. In a study by two Harvard psychologists, subjects were willing to take as much as a 25 percent pay cut just to share their opinions.[7]

Creating your Communication Compact ensures that sharing information and opinions doesn't disrupt the chain of command yet allows for the most efficient flow in communication to help employees get their work done rather than wait on approvals and feedback. Effective Communication Compacts address two critical ways organizations communicate in the digital age: messaging and meetings. The next two chapters explore how to succeed with both.

CHAPTER 15

Digital Communication: E-mail, Messaging, and Everything in Between

I t's early morning, and an employee of yours awakens to the sound of the mail truck pulling up. Putting on slippers, she walks to her mailbox, retrieves its contents, and thumbs through her letters, magazines, and ads on the way back inside.

Not 20 seconds later, the mail truck pulls up behind her in the driveway. As she turns around, the letter carrier runs up and says, "There's more!" He hands her another pile, then asks if she's responded to any of the mail he dropped off just a few moments ago.

If e-mail were physical, this is what it would look like. Most of it is noise. But because some messages could actually be important, your employee trudges through it.

Pulling up e-mail on our smartphones every morning is like returning from a vacation to find more than a hundred pieces of mail waiting for us.

How do we turn down the volume?

CONNECTED BUT DISCONNECTED

Your employee is sitting at her son's swim meet, checking e-mail. Adrenaline shudders through her but not because of the race. It's because of a note from you with a red exclamation mark.

The sound of cheering jolts her back to the meet. Her son just beat his own record in the 200-meter freestyle. Sadly, the first chance she'll get to see it is when another mom posts the video to Facebook that night.

E-mail might have freed us from the time and hassle of snail mail and fax machines. But it has also shackled us to our phones and made sustaining focus on important things much harder.

But it's not going away anytime soon. Nor do we want it to.

BRING THE NOISE

We like the noise. We check our work e-mail in bed because, hey, we can check our work e-mail in bed.

E-mail and messaging are efficient and quick, and they provide a record of communication, which is especially important when you're leading others. How much easier is it to text a quick work request than to call the person, maybe risking a wake-up or conversation neither of you needs to have?

One sentence. Done.

But all this convenience has created a sprawling monster. Not just e-mail, but every kind of messaging.

Imagine that your e-mail somehow breaks. After you've loudly cursed your fate, a colleague texts you to say his e-mail to you bounced. Another colleague sends an IM. Your best friend direct messages you on Twitter. And Mom was worried, so she left a note on Facebook. In other words, everyone can still get in touch with you.

I've seen companies try to replace e-mail only to see their digital volume increase.

One of my clients was a business consultant for a major telecom whose cure for e-mail volume was worse than the disease. Their integrated internal messaging system worked *too* well: Employees spent all day talking on it instead of doing their jobs.

The old paradigm of removing barriers, in this case, unleashed a new distraction. The telecom didn't pay enough attention to the "why" of its spiffy new technology: improving communication and productivity.

The challenge for all digital communication, whether it's e-mail, a messaging app, or some new channel that hasn't been invented yet, is *improving quality* and *reducing quantity*.

IMPROVING QUALITY

Quality isn't about perfection—in fact, digital communication is a great example for where perfect can be the enemy of good.

Digital communication needs to be clear, but it also exists for recording and efficiency. Writing perfectly, and expecting others to do so, *undermines* efficiency. Yes, I just said it. I'm writing about e-mail quality and starting by actually lining up on the side of those who write in incomplete sentences, abbreviations, and emojis. Don't get me wrong. There's a time for writing that resembles a Victorian-age letter, but let's not compare someone who wrote one letter a week to people who are expected to respond to more than 50 messages a day. If you are writing an important e-mail to a client, then get it right. Otherwise, the keys to quality in digital communication are clarity and utility.

Spelling and grammar matter, of course, but they aren't primary goals. Much better for you and your people to focus on clear messaging, leaving the rest to apps like Grammarly that automatically find and correct your typos.

Check out the following tips from the *Harvard Business Review*.[1]

Use Keywords in Subject Lines

The purpose of an e-mail should be immediately clear. The military uses subject line keywords, including:

- ACTION—recipient has to take some action
- SIGN—signature required
- INFO—no response needed
- DECISION—a decision is needed
- REQUEST—permission or approval is needed

"INFO—Status update" and "REQUEST—Medical leave" will stand out in a person's inbox. Writing clear subject lines also compels us to consider what we really need from someone before adding to his or her inbox clutter.

Put the Important Stuff First

Journalism students are admonished not to bury the lead—that is, delay what matters most in a story. Effective e-mail quickly hits the five W's: who, what, where, when, and why. Without excess information, it answers the question of how does this e-mail affect me?

Here's an example:

Subject: INFO—Sick days

Paul,

Bottom line: Effective January 1, employees can bank just three days of sick time from the previous year, down from the current five.

Background:

- This is an effort to increase productivity by reducing the temptation to take sick days for nonmedical purposes.

- The leadership team supported the decision.

Paul knows right away that no response is needed because of "INFO" in the subject line. The bottom line gets to the point quickly, and the background makes clear that the decision is final, backed by management, and intended to boost productivity.

Be Economical

Short e-mails are most effective, so try to fit everything in one pane to spare the recipient from having to scroll. To save space, and boost clarity, use active rather than passive voice. Put nouns first so that verbs can do the work.

No: The off-site was organized by Sue.

Yes: Sue organized the off-site.

Here's a nifty trick from the well-known blogger James Altucher: Try deleting every other sentence when you write.[2] Although not something that always applies, it's a great test. And it's amazing how often you can, in fact, do it without losing anything.

Also, linking to attachments rather than attaching files prevents inbox (and hard drive) clutter. A website or internal network will likely have the most recent version of a file. Plus, the site can verify that the recipient has the proper credentials to see it.

Last thing: Quit thinking old school and use emojis already. They're an essential stand-in for expressed emotion, body language, and other aspects of face-to-face communication.[3] According to one study, we accurately differentiate seriousness from sarcasm over e-mail only 56 percent of the time.[4] A smile emoji can go a long way toward showing intent and reducing conflict. With that said, here's a public service announcement: Confirm the emoji's accepted meaning prior to use. A client was sure a certain emoji was chocolate ice cream. He loved chocolate ice cream! His clients were...confused. It wasn't chocolate ice cream.

REDUCING QUANTITY

Turning down the e-mail volume is an organization-wide effort. Below are some tips for you and your team.

Move Communication to the Platform Where the Work Belongs

As we discussed in Section 4, it's counterproductive to send key information about a project with an e-mail program that distracts from working on the project. Communicate in the project-management program. Make this expectation part of your Communication

Compact. (And if your project-management program doesn't offer easy ways to communicate within the platform, it's time to upgrade.)

Limit Announcements

I worked with a company where every sale sparked a team-wide announcement. For a staff of 60 salespeople, that meant 15 to 20 *ding-ding-dings* a day. It was fun and encouraging at first, but soon everyone stopped paying attention.

How about one catchall e-mail at the end of the day? Or, better yet, an announcement posted to a physical bulletin board that everyone sees.

Stop Hitting Send So Much

The best way to receive fewer e-mails is to—yep, you guessed it—send fewer e-mails. Shocking. I know. Don't broadcast every half-formed idea or ask about minor things you can address in person.

Here's how: You can drastically reduce your e-mail load by simply asking two questions.

1. Do I really need to send this?
2. How can I write this to reduce the likelihood of a future e-mail that needs a response?

Oftentimes, an e-mail chain goes like this:

You: Want to jump on a call to chat about this?

Them: Sure!

You: What times work well for you?

Them: Next week is open . . .

. . . and 14 e-mails later, you have a plan.

A focus-wise e-mail goes like this: "I would love to discuss this by phone. Are you available at any of the following times? [list dates]

If so, send me a confirmation of the best time and I will call you at [phone number]. If not, send me three alternative options for me to confirm."

And help others by telling them "FYI" or "no response needed"; or, better yet, group adopt the short-form INFO listed previously.

Move to BCC

I'm not sure when it happened, but it seems most of corporate America has contracted the CC virus. It's spread and infested businesses and teams across the planet. It's a veritable pandemic, and it's time to kill it.

Being CC'd consigns your recipient (and yourself) to "reply all" purgatory—an endless string of unnecessary responses. This not only increases volume, but it also buries the replies you actually need to see.

If your goal is for everyone to know who is informed, just list the people who received the message in the e-mail.

Reply in Chunks

Schedule times to look at e-mail instead of peeking every time you hear the alert (in fact: turn off the alert). You don't need to know when an e-mail arrives. Less checking means less channel-switching. Or simply shut off your e-mail program until you're ready for it again (yes, you can actually do that).

This doesn't mean you can't glance at your e-mail when walking between meetings (because that's what walks are for, right?). But scheduling time to answer e-mails in bulk will save you time and help you do your best work.

Don't Expect Immediate Responses

Set aside a communication channel that isn't primarily for work and that can be used in an emergency. Rather than assuming all e-mail is an emergency, maybe your team can agree that actual emergencies will result in a phone call or a text (a form of communication that isn't used in bulk).

Also, make emergencies the exception rather than the rule. If I get a call from my wife, I know I need to answer. If I get a text, I reply as needed. Same goes from a message from my team.

I will offer one caveat here: There are people whose role does truly require them to be available and responsive at all times—and that's okay. The key is to make sure that those positions are reserved for distinct roles—such as executive admins—and not assumed for all roles. These roles serve as connections for reaching executives in an emergency so that they are not beholden to all channels at all times. They can have vault time too, knowing that they are still available to those who need to reach them without being interrupted by an e-mail announcing the flash deal on blenders.

Bonus Tip for Leaders: Schedule or Save Drafts to Send Later

Just because you're e-mailing late at night doesn't mean your team needs to read your brilliance right away. Tools such as Boomerang allow you to schedule e-mail delivery in Gmail and Outlook (saving attention resources since you won't have to remember to send a message later). Or simply save messages to your drafts folder until office hours to relieve the burden on employees during off-hours.

Your drafts folder can serve another purpose: templates. E-mail templates save you time from writing e-mails you frequently reuse, particularly those where quality includes grammar and persuasion rather than simply clarity and efficiency.

I have a template e-mail that includes several versions of requests for information about our services. Another provides postevent follow-up to event planners. I grab the template that best fits, then customize accordingly. This saves not minutes but hours.

By putting these tips into practice, you'll create a vibrant workplace that cuts the clutter and turns down the volume. Your employees will get clarity on what's important, complete work more efficiently, and best of all, be happier.

CHAPTER 16

Face to Face in a Facebook World

As part of an $80 million condo conversion, a colleague of mine once managed three units: sales, leasing, and construction. Leasing was in the main clubhouse, sales in a converted unit, and construction in another converted unit. Between them all was a pool.

The project was complex, and deadlines were tight. As a result, digital communication led to huge conflicts, spawning epic e-mail chains, even though everyone was no more than 30 to 100 feet apart. So, the company instituted a policy called "walk across the pond" (the pool). If communication required more than three e-mails, employees would walk across the pond and talk.

Relationships and productivity dramatically improved.

FACE TIME (NOT THE iPHONE KIND)

People don't want to talk face to face. This isn't a generational issue. It's a human issue.

Digital communication is easier because we're hardwired to avoid conflict and we like control. At work, we can rationalize the convenience of reaching people quickly or that much of our team is never in the office anyway. Our brains, however, are also cocooning us from unpleasantness. That terse, one-word (with a period, no less!) answer to an e-mail seems so innocent in digital form, but imagine giving the same answer in person at a meeting. You'd probably be able to cut through the tension with a knife.

Constant connection creates digital distance. And that is bad for your team. Why? For one thing, we risk isolation. This seems counterintuitive, right? Constant connection should make us feel more, well, connected. If you can communicate digitally on your own terms at your own time, you should get the community without the inconvenience. Except not.

In the 1980s, 20 percent of adults surveyed described themselves as lonely; today, that number is 40 percent.[1] Research also suggests isolation disrupts sleep, alters the immune system, causes more inflammation and stress, and increases the risk of premature death by 14 percent.[2]

As David Brooks talks about in one of my favorite books of all time, *The Social Animal*, humans are made to be truly connected—to be social:

> Your unconscious, that inner extrovert, wants you to reach outward and connect. It wants you to achieve communion with work, friend, family, nation, and cause. Your unconscious wants to entangle you in the thick web of relations that are the essence of human flourishing. It longs and pushes for love.... Of all the blessings that come with being alive, it is the most awesome gift.[3]

Digital interactions inoculate us from complete isolation through shallow connection and dopamine rewards, making us think we can avoid the messiness that comes from authentic communication and connection—until we look up and realize we are in fact experiencing a hollowed-out version.

Worse, perhaps, is that we struggle to empathize in the digital wilderness. As comments posted on social media show, cruelty is much easier from a distance (a problem that bleeds into the office).

We are engineered for empathy, a process that begins with mirror neurons. They're the cornerstone of what causes us to reflect and experience the emotions we see in others.[4]

When I smile, your brain lights up as if you're smiling. When I yawn, you yawn. When I'm sad, you understand that sadness because your brain feels it.

We don't like negative feelings. When we offend someone, we automatically feel their emotions through our mirror neurons. (Less risk of that, our brains tell us, with digital communication.) In other words, we're hardwired when a friend asks, "Do I look fat?" to say, "Of course not!" Empathy, in short, helps us play well with others. On the other hand, we have no problem using Twitter—where the consequences of mirror neurons are removed—to call an actress we don't know ugly (just Google "mean tweets" if you don't believe me).

As leaders, we must sometimes lift communication beyond the digital. That means fighting what feels easiest and helping your teams to do the same. But when should in-person communication be utilized? When efficiency and emotional connection demand it.

EFFICIENCY

We'll often prolong an argument electronically rather than walk across the pond for an in-person chat.

Sometimes we choose digital inefficiency because it offers less pain, more control, and dopamine without discomfort. In the meantime, problems are buried in a blizzard of reply all.

That's why it's often more efficient to get up and talk with a person than to prolong an IM conversation that keeps both of you from doing real work.

In-person communication can also be more effective for group conversations—yes, meetings. True, they're about as popular as spam, and as we discussed earlier, they often do waste time and money. (I worked with a COO who added up the wages of people attending a two-hour meeting. It totaled more than $20,000.)

Meetings Gone Awesome

Still, meetings are a necessary part of work, providing space for collaboration, coordination, relationship building, and celebration. They usually go awry because someone in charge didn't consider one of these tips.

Have a Clear Purpose. Is the meeting still fulfilling its original purpose? (Often, we keep meetings on the calendar even when they're no longer useful.) Is this the best way to communicate the information in question?

Be Realistic But Constrictive about Time. Meetings will fill the time allotted. Is it being used efficiently? A lot can be covered in a short duration; my colleagues and I often meet for 20 minutes.

Meet in the Afternoon. In general, groups create focus when individual focus is waning, such as in the afternoon. Try to schedule meetings when people would otherwise struggle to focus on their own.

Make Sure Everyone Shows Up. Is everyone who needs to be involved present? If not, you're wasting time. Rethink "attendance is mandatory."

Case in point: I was just on a scheduled conference call where we found out the key person couldn't make it. Rather than reschedule, someone suggested we start the conversation and then have another when the person was available. That's translation for, "We can have a dress rehearsal without the leading role in attendance." No, we can't. Cancel. Reschedule. Save time and money.

Prepare an Agenda. Without one, your meetings will flounder. No agenda, no attenda! This is particularly important for the growing necessity of catchall/catchup meetings.

Don't Expect Preparation. I heard anecdotally that Jeff Bezos takes 5 minutes at the start so his team can read up on whatever the meeting is about. He acknowledges what we all know: No one comes prepared.

Clear the Clutter. For one-on-one and small-group meetings, start by letting people quickly share what's on their mind. That way, your agenda can get full attention. Even if it means spending a little more time on what someone else is thinking about, you end up, as a group, being more efficient because you gave your team the chance to clear the clutter in their minds and focus on the tasks at hand.

Establish Rules for Tech. Does technology help or hinder the meeting? Are there clear rules for usage? Should phones and laptops be allowed? It's amazing how much secondary conflict I hear about other people's tech behavior during meetings. This is a primary way the Communication Compact can help.

Going tech-free may be neither realistic nor desirable (I type way faster than I write). But you can still set parameters for phones (off when full focus is required) and laptops (closed unless their use contributes to the meeting).

An extra word on phones: If they're not allowed, make sure team members know in advance. You can also schedule breaks for phone use (sometimes a client can't wait).

Who Types the Fastest? Assign someone to take notes. This means fewer people need to use their laptops.

EMOTIONAL CONNECTION

A colleague of mine once filled in for a supervisor on maternity leave. His peers became jealous of him, particularly because he had little managerial experience. He felt like he had to manage with a heavy hand. Eventually, the tension between him and the team boiled to a point that he finally addressed it with his team, and he started crying. It wasn't planned, and it wasn't comfortable.

But you know what? The dam of resentment broke, my colleague eased up, and the team ran like a Swiss watch afterward.

"There's no crying in baseball!" Tom Hanks's character famously tells a weeping player in *A League of Their Own*. Maybe for good reason. Maybe not.

We have mixed emotions about emotions. Especially in the workplace, and even without e-mail and texting. My colleague addressed his team at the dawn of digital communication. Imagine if he had tried to do so on an e-mail string.

The only way to experience emotional empathy like the kind my colleague experienced is through in-person interaction—that's what sparks the mirror neuron magic.

Otherwise, we're forced to use a process called cognitive empathy, which comes from the prefrontal cortex, our "thinking" brain. In lieu of an auto-response from seeing and hearing emotions in person, we can access cognitive empathy by intentionally asking, "How will people feel when they read this e-mail?"

But cognitive empathy is a complicated, time-consuming, and exhausting mental process (using more glucose, the brain energy discussed in Chapter 6). It's the path of most resistance. Add stress and a lack of sleep, and we're less likely to restrain our frustration in the digital realm.

Our response to a rude e-mail early in the day might be diplomatic. Later on, there's a better chance it will be snarky. "Sleep on it" is not just wisdom; it's straight-up biology. (Type that e-mail response now, but review it in the morning before hitting send.)

Digital communication requires us to use cognitive empathy—something even the most emotionally intelligent among us don't have the ability to do well when our energy reserves are low. That's why we should seek opportunities to connect face to face so we can employ emotional empathy, particularly for the following kinds of interactions.

Critical Conversations

Refrain from having deep conversations via e-mail, text, or even the phone. There are simply too many avenues for misunderstanding.

Taking the time to meet with employees frames your respect for them and the importance of what you're discussing. It's never been easier to avoid face-to-face conversations. It's never been more critical not to.

Conflict

Your worth as a leader is often defined by how you handle conflict. Digital communication avoids honest and empathetic discussion, increasing conflict before banishing it to an endless e-mail string. The result is some of your team's best work is squashed. Conflict can actually be quite healthy, if processed correctly, for innovation. Resolving conflict must begin with the leader. Author Edwin Friedman writes of the dangers of leaders shirking their responsibility to face conflict in *A Failure of Nerve: Leadership in the Age of the Quick Fix*, which was privately published in 1999, three years after his death:

> In any type of institution whatsoever, when a self-directed, imaginative, energetic, or creative member is being consistently frustrated and sabotaged rather than encouraged and supported, what will turn out to be true one hundred percent of the time, regardless of whether the disrupters are supervisors, subordinates, or peers, is that the person at the very top of that institution is a peace-monger. By that I mean a highly anxious risk-avoider, someone who is more concerned with good feelings than with progress, someone whose life revolves around the axis of consensus, a "middler," someone who is so incapable of taking well-defined stands that his "disability" seems to be genetic, someone who functions as if she had been filleted of her backbone, someone who treats conflict or anxiety like mustard gas—one whiff, on goes the emotional gas mask, and he flits. Such leaders are often "nice," if not charming.[5]

Leadership means engagement, not avoidance. It means doing the right thing, not just being "nice." Set a cultural expectation that conflicts will be handled in person. Your team—and your company—will thank you for it.

Syncs

Early on in my business, I aimed for efficiency by having every member of the team focus only on their particular area (with me being the only person who knew all that was taking place). Unfortunately, I also dealt with several employees frustrated by other team members and by their own compensation (because when you know only about your work, you think you are doing all the work!).

I shared my cultural struggles with a dear friend, Patrick Riley, the CEO of Global Accelerator Network, in hopes that he could offer some solution for the constant battle of everyone thinking they should own the company. He explained that the fastest route to making people stop overvaluing their own role was to let them see what everyone else is doing. So, we started meeting as a group for quick syncs. I learned that this seeming "inefficiency" was essential to the health of a small, growing team.

The important lesson I learned is that team members can become so siloed that they fail to grasp the importance of other roles. Syncs (relax, they're not meetings) allow them to see the big picture and share what they do while hearing what others do. This increases understanding and reduces entitlement.

At Microsoft, employees have shared their work in "5-minute downloads." These short presentations enlighten the team about individual roles, removing mystery and emphasizing value.

Team-Building

I'm often asked to speak at team-building events. In one example, a company that sells high-tech research equipment knew its employees felt disconnected. So the leadership flew the entire sales team from all over the world to Florida.

The four-day event cost $1 million but more than recouped its cost in improved morale, collaboration, and productivity. There's no substitute for in-person, off-site gatherings to refresh and refocus your team.

Motivational Talks

Not long ago, conferences seemed headed for oblivion. It was the primary subject of virtually every meeting's industry dialogue. Alas, conference doomsdayers couldn't have been more wrong. They failed to understand that the rise of digital communication actually increased the demand for intentional face-to-face contact.

That's why conferences, and speaker fees, are on the rise. A great speaker can engage employees in a way that no digital medium can. This is, in part, because mirror neurons are in effect. But there is a caveat here: The speaker has to be really great. Live audiences don't have patience for the equivalent of Ben Stein in *Ferris Bueller's Day Off*. Nothing can beat the value of a dynamic speaker, which is why spending $15,000 on a speech that doesn't waste your team's time and helps them get motivated feels like a no-brainer. Am I biased on this point? Probably. Am I wrong? Not at all.

Motivation, however, starts with us as leaders. An in-person presentation allows us to do what no e-mail can: establish (or reestablish) our persona and credibility and connect emotionally with our team. Hone your communication skills, and subsequently train your people to be great communicators.

Communication Compact Discussion

Finally, the discussion we talked about in Chapter 14 is absolutely critical for any of the rest of this to have a shot. You must meet in person once a year to discuss how you can improve internal communication, set ground rules and accountability, and remind each other you are all on the same page seeking the same goal.

Miscommunication is part of life. But it can destroy a company as quickly as it can destroy a marriage. Setting time aside to spotlight these and rectify them is an essential and unique need in the age of constant connectivity and increased isolation.

So go ahead and get that meeting on the books now, before you read on.

NOW THAT I HAVE YOUR ATTENTION...

For Section 5 reflection questions, summary video, and next step resources, please visit focuswise.com/book

FOCUS-WISE WORKDAY

CHAPTER **17**

The Balance Myth

A friend of mine worked the constantly connected workplace to her advantage until it worked her into the ground. She was a rising star at a major consulting firm who, like many in her profession, put in countless hours and made herself available 24/7.

Her husband intervened after discovering she was setting her alarm for 1 and 3 AM to reply to e-mails, then getting up again at about 5 AM. She averaged three to four hours of sleep a night.

Her salary was ridiculous—but so was her life, if you could call it that. Eventually, not even a 50 percent raise could make her stay at the firm.

Now she coaches her kid's basketball team—and quite happily so.

Abetted by technology, we live in a culture that encourages us to speed past the semblance of a balanced life. Some jobs flat out demand this speed, and a great many of us *like it.*

Overworking becomes welded to our identity, part of "an age where talent, passion, and authenticity are hailed as virtues and antidotes to the uncertainty of the workplace."[1] Work becomes a kind of romance filled with the same turbulence. Even if we reject the romance for ourselves, we encourage our employees to fall in love. If you know anything about welding, you can see the problem. Welding literally fuses things together so they can't be undone without breaking or cutting the weld off. Once overworking is what others expect of you, and what you expect from yourself, it can be difficult to step back.

I sold my house earlier this year. My real estate agent, a friend, was extremely driven, painfully focused, and—no surprise—highly successful. She worked late into the night posting pictures, videos, and marketing materials in every corner of cyberspace.

I loved it. She never said, "I'll work on that after my kid's school play." For all I knew, she never saw her kids. All that mattered to me, honestly, was how she hustled to sell my house.

Aren't these the people we want working for us?

"Yes, I expect people to work however long it takes," an executive from a consulting company told me. "There's a long line of people waiting for the chance to work here. If they want to spend more time on the ski slopes, then go be a lift operator. I pay them well and expect them to work accordingly."

Leaders increasingly demand this kind of work ethic, even when it's not in tune with the people they hire. According to an Oxford Economics study, more than half of employees described work-life balance as important to them, but only a third of executives agreed it was a priority for their people.[2] That's a massive gap.

Maybe that's why some countries are stepping in to regulate what exactly businesses can mandate. France, for example, has enacted a law requiring companies with 50 or more workers to write a charter protecting the right to disconnect from digital communication outside of regular business hours.[3]

This approach is wonderfully intentioned and probably unworkable, and it will most likely result in negative and unintended consequences. Whatever government-mandated digital cutoffs look like, they are not true work-life balance. So what does it look like?

SEPARATING WORK AND LIFE

The answer is that we don't really know. That's because, like unicorns, work-life balance doesn't exist.

Even the phrase *work-life balance* sounds off—like something out of George Orwell's *Nineteen Eighty-Four*, a world in which much of the language means its opposite. Think twice when a prospective employer touts work-life balance. It might very well mean working nights and weekends. Then again, it might mean leaving the office at 4 PM and partaking in 3 PM Friday happy hour each week, which is nice unless you actually want to compete.

Work-life balance was coined to describe a problem that can't be solved. But that's okay—because it doesn't need to be. Balance isn't the goal. The goal is to thrive both at work and home by proactively knowing when to separate and when to intermingle the two.

How often do experts go to the extreme when addressing work-life balance in an article or speech? I've seen earnest people preach total separation between the two: At 6 PM, I turn off my phone and don't look at it until 8 AM the next day.

That's just not realistic. What if a task dominates your thoughts? Is it wrong to devote 15 minutes to focused work at home so you can truly relax with friends that evening?

What if a vital conference call can only be scheduled at 7:30 PM? How unreasonable would it be to go home at 4:30, hang out with the family, then retreat to your home office for an hour? Technology can make working at home really convenient.

The total separation approach also migrates to the office: No personal calls or texts. I block out the world and focus only on work.

Okay then. Tough luck if you need to call your tax guy about a looming audit because he leaves at 5. Maybe he'll pick up his phone on Saturday.

And you can answer your wife's text about whether to buy tickets for a popular show . . . after it sells out.

The reality is that work-life balance is one of our culture's most beloved and misguided myths.

For most of us, work and life are inextricably intertwined (and what technology has joined together, let no man separate). We can, however, learn to be proactive in how we approach the intertwining—rather than reacting to whatever each demands. We can be the sailboat instead of the raft.

The raft rises and dips in a helpless dance with its environment. A sailboat harnesses the same winds and currents to productive ends. A raft you just sit on. A sailboat you steer and keep balanced. There is a tension when sailing that doesn't exist on a raft, and the same is true with life. We must become comfortable living within the tension of knowing we might achieve rare moments of balance but that the bulk of our existence is swaying back and forth and intermingling between the various roles we play.

Is it freeing to realize that the cultural expectations placed on us are totally unrealistic? Today's *homo distractus* is expected to give 100 percent in every sphere of life. And she feels guilty that she isn't giving enough to any. You need to be the best employee. And you need to be the best parent. That means hitting all soccer games. Be home when the kids get home. Don't be a slave to work. Then again, you aren't a great parent if your company goes belly up or you get fired. See the tension?

We would do well to listen to musician, filmmaker, entrepreneur, Venture Capitalist, and dear friend Ben Patterson: "Balance is the lie that says, 'I can do everything.' There is no balance. But there is a convergence of priorities that is primarily defined by what I say no to."

We constantly need to adjust our footing to meet the demands of the moment. Sometimes, work requires more. And that's okay. Sometimes we need to take a day off to recalibrate with our family. And that's okay too.

So what does this mean for a leader, given the roles our people play in the constantly connected workplace?

Captaining the Ship

As a leader, you are in a unique position to both captain your own sailboat and help your people captain theirs. The following principles will help you and your team navigate the tensions between work and life.

The Fastest Runner Sets the Pace. If you, as the leader, have not explicitly set expectations for how your team should approach work, the person who replies fastest and works longest will be the standard bearer. The Oxford study also revealed that 26 percent of executives expected employees to be available after hours, whereas 46 percent of employees considered this the expectation. That's a big gap in perception.

Even if you don't require people to stay after hours, other employees might create this culture. And you will unknowingly allow a culture of constant responsiveness and availability at a cost you might not realize.

Always Available Means Never Fully Available. Overworked employees aren't effective employees. Everyone needs downtime to recharge—away from work.

A dear friend led operations for a successful recruiting firm. He started as the CEO's personal assistant but evolved into the person who ran the entire organization. He worked 80 hours a week. To free up his own focus, the CEO asked my friend to manage an endless stream of inputs. Every single request to the CEO went through my friend. Rather than systemize the business, this CEO made my friend the system. The CEO was appreciative—he showered him with frequent high-priced gifts, such as an iPad and (short) beach vacations, and made sure he was compensated well. But the situation wasn't sustainable, and over time, resentment grew inside my friend as his life took a backseat to, well, everything. Eventually, he quit, which came as a huge blow to the CEO. When my friend told him he was leaving, the CEO pleaded, "Just tell me the number!" There was no number. He now teaches biology and couldn't be happier.

Leaders tend to measure productivity by 1) task completion and 2) time spent working (and the bonus goes to the person who stays late and replies on the weekends). What they're not measuring is employee burnout and high replacement and turnover costs.

There is a popular belief that 24/7 availability and immediate response times are the requirement for high-octane organizations. Here's the actual truth: Experiments in which organizations have curtailed messaging (off-hours and at work) have led to happier, more relaxed employees. Low-value output shrinks (along with work hours!), but the important stuff still gets done.[4] It's a classic example of slowing down to speed up.

There's another hidden cost to the always-available employee mindset. When employees are always available, they are forced to channel-switch and adopt the one-person-band lifestyle, switching constantly between spheres—and diminishing their contribution in each of them.

Ironically, always-available employees overvalue their contribution and justify working less when they are supposed to be working fully. It's much easier to justify 45 minutes on IM with a might-be love interest when you can say, "I answer e-mails at 8 PM anyway."

As leaders, we need to consider our people's longevity and their focus. That starts with creating a climate in which employees can realize the expectation is to prioritize and focus on the right things at the right time. This will mean defining levels of access (more on that to come).

Nine to Five Is So Last Century. An Oregon State University study found that a healthy sex life boosts job satisfaction.[5] No, I'm not suggesting we adopt a policy of adding "How's the sex life?" to the annual review, but I am suggesting that our team members' personal lives spill over into work. The world where work and life were separated is gone—there is no returning to it. That means you have to be a leader who walks the narrow line between infringing upon privacy while being empathetic and aware that the way your team manages this tension will directly impact their effectiveness on the job.

As leaders, we need to take an interest in employees beyond what happens between 9 and 5. The truth is there are no simple answers on how to do this well, and there are unintended consequences to all approaches. I've found the most effective approach is to be a leader who is empathetic, aware, and intentional about valuing the "other half" of life but who also creates enough personal separation to allow for the hard conversations to take place when needed. You shouldn't be your employees' best friend, but on the other hand, if you don't know their kids' names, you're just kind of a jerk.

NOT EITHER/OR BUT IF/THEN

Rather than fixate on work-life balance, you should think in terms of degrees of access—being intentional with to whom, how much, and when we are accessible. Most people simply don't think this way. Like we discussed earlier, the temptation is to think you need to give 100 percent to a hundred different things, which is actually 10,000 percent . . . and impossible.

Being focus-wise means actively assigning availability based on your degree of access. That mode will depend on circumstances and context. It's also important to make sure that those who rely on you, at work and at home, understand what mode you're in.

At Focuswise, we developed a system that helps you define and manage your levels of access (Figure 17.1). The following are the three levels of access and when to use them. To be clear, these are not either/or choices but rather if/then choices. There will be times where you need to operate in each degree of access. The key to success is knowing the right time and communicating it to all who need to know.

Level A: Total Block

In this mode, nothing exists but the work in front of you or the family around you, for instance. No distractions from the other sphere, be it e-mail, social media, or phone calls.

Total block requires a Communication Compact at work and at home. You must assign time for this level—it simply won't happen naturally.

For example, a friend of mine is having a baby soon. He has worked with his team to assign all his responsibilities for coverage during the two weeks he'll be at home with his new baby. Additionally, his manager has agreed to cover any crises or big decisions that need to be made while he is out. As far as his employer is concerned, he will be totally blocked out. His team knows it, and everyone is ready to support it. This planning ahead will be key to him enjoying the time with his family and not worrying about work.

But this shouldn't be just reserved for emergencies. You can build this level of access into your daily or weekly calendar for each sphere of life that matters to you. For instance, my wife and I have a time each night where we go for a walk after dinner. It's just us, the dogs, and the kids. No phones. No interruptions.

Put simply: If something really matters to you, then being fully present within it for a sustained period of time is a must.

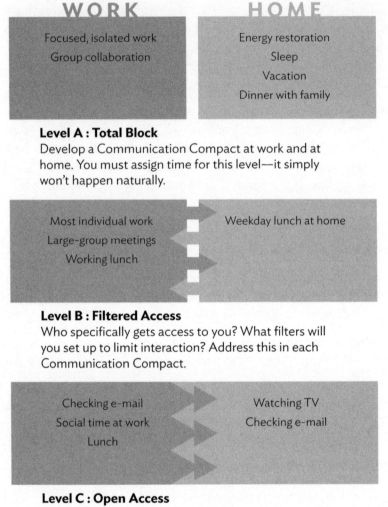

Figure 17.1   Access Management Guide.

Level B: Filtered Access

This is where you set up filters limiting access at specific times. At work, for instance, turn on the do not disturb feature for your phone and e-mail during a project, but leave Slack on so that people on the project can reach you. Or perhaps you don't check texts or e-mail while in a weekly sync, but a phone call from the spouse is important and worth stepping out of the meeting. Either way, the question is: Who specifically gets access to you?

It's this question that forms the key difference between a healthy approach to separating and integrating the various spheres of our work and lives. Most people simply assume open access. But filtered access is a new requirement of the focus-wise in the age of constant connectivity. And the method you use to implement this is the Communication Compact.

Perhaps the most common example of this is when someone leaves the office at 4 PM for a personal errand but says, "I'm available by Slack or text if something important comes up." The person is exercising flexibility by doing a personal task during work hours but setting up a filter that allows access should something that needs to be addressed in a timely manner come up.

Personally, my wife and I have a Communication Compact around texts during work hours. She knows I will respond if I have free time, but she doesn't expect it. It's been discussed and agreed upon.

If she immediately needs me for something, however, she calls me. This happens maybe once a month. I will step out of meetings for her call. I will not step off a stage from a speech, though, because that's a total block time. She knows if I don't answer, that means a total block. She can either escalate to my director of operations or (as is almost always the case) leave a voicemail knowing her need is top priority as soon as I see it.

Level C: Open Access

Professionals spend most of their time in this mode. Open access is okay sometimes but not as a default. Otherwise, you're constantly pushing off on a raft, tossed about by distractions at work and at home.

Open access works great when you're doing things that don't require your full attention, either with family, friends, or work. These things could be replying to routine e-mails, having a catchup call with a friend, watching a baseball game on TV, browsing Facebook, or enjoying a happy hour with the team. If my wife texts me during this time, I'm answering. If my kid wants to wrestle, I'll do it with the ball game still on.

Sometimes, however, the importance of timing can also trump other levels of access—but only for a short period. It should never be the norm.

For instance, imagine you're working with your team on an important pitch to a client. It's getting right up to the time of the meeting and there's still a lot of work to be done. This deal could make or break the coming fiscal year. You better believe that if someone needs to get ahold of you, they can.

Personally, as the deadline for this book comes quickly, the team working on it with me is in constant communication at all times, day and night. That includes open access at home during time typically reserved for family. This means that though I usually limit home access, it doesn't make sense to do so now. It's just a short period of time—and a necessary one. Once the book is done, everything will reset to normal, which is most of the time Level B.

In fact, the most successful people I know embrace Level B. They filter out distractions for focused work but also take breaks for family, friends, colleagues, and unavoidable interruptions.

All three levels of access are necessary for success in the workplace today. But they should be exercised only at the appropriate time, and everyone should understand the rules of the game. Discuss expectations with your team and give them the tools for focused work throughout the day. Take a similar approach at home. And make sure you develop Communication Compacts for both parts of your life.

How to Assign the Areas in Your Life a Level

Now that you know the levels, you can assign the various areas of your life and work into the level. Here's how:

- Write down the major spheres of your life (work, home, social, personal, community/church).

- For each sphere, make a list of the major activities and who is involved in each. It's helpful to refer to your calendar. You don't need to get too specific. If you watch *Game of Thrones* one night and basketball the next, just label it *evening TV*.

- Reorganize the activities in order of importance.

Designate Level A, B, or C for each activity.

- For each Level B category, answer the question: Who gets let in and how?

- For Levels A and B: What tools need to be in place? What conversations do I need to have?

Moving forward, include the access level when you add activities to your calendar.

BLURRED LINES

My first job was cleaning up on a construction site. At work, I worked. At home, I played video games and talked with my girlfriend for hours on the phone. The separation was clear.

This year, my wife and I had a house built, meaning frequent visits to the construction site. A framer, 15 feet in the air and balanced on two beams, answered his phone. The fireplace installer showed me countless designs floating across the screen of an iPad that no doubt contained personal e-mail and pictures of his kids. The landscaper e-mailed plans in the middle of the night while on vacation in Florida.

Today, the separation is far from clear.

Work isn't just work, and home isn't just home. Our people are navigating both worlds 24/7, and many of them need our help.

That starts with adopting a focus-wise approach to delineation and delegation.

CHAPTER 18

Managing the Minutiae

You settle into your desk at work, wake up your laptop, and scan today's to-do list. Fifty-four items. *A little light today.*

In reality, you're not going to get 54 things done during the workday, but tackling some of these tasks means *not* tackling others. Which means they'll haunt you on tomorrow's list, which probably already includes items from last year.

Who invented the stupid to-do list anyway?

Today's worker is drowning in to-dos. The volume of tasks you and your employees must manage leads to an inevitable sense of overload. Sixty-four percent of workers younger than age 34 report feeling overwhelmed at work. So do 59 percent of their colleagues ages 35 to 54.[1]

Task lists continue to grow in the constantly connected workplace, forcing us to differentiate each task's importance. But how do we know where to start?

Most workers let their inboxes dictate importance or let their to-do lists assign equal value to every item. Either way, most of us attack the easy stuff first.

This morning, I had 67 e-mails, a flight itinerary to review, some personal accounting, three phone calls, and this chapter to write. The latter required the most focus. So, of course, I was tempted to handle e-mails, book travel, and make my calls first. Dopamine flows when we check off lots of little items on our lists.

But the most important item was the chapter. Almost every other task could have waited until after lunch and my post-carbohydrate drag.

My answer to the temptation was something I aptly label my *warmup lap*. I quickly checked e-mail, made a prioritized list, and even knocked out a few easy and time-sensitive items to get moving. It didn't take me very long, and wasn't a bottomless pit of procrastination, but it got me mentally ready to *really* work. Then I tackled the chapter.

The key to the warmup lap, however, is to make sure it's really just a warmup and not a full marathon. During a recent talk I gave in Scottsdale, Arizona, I wanted to hike the famous Camelback Mountain. It looked pretty close to my hotel, so I thought, *Why not jog to it and then hike up?* Turns out large objects look close by for a long time. I ended up doing a long run to get a great Instagram photo of me near (or I think near) the mountain followed by a long jog back to the hotel. I never got to the hike because I wasted all my resources on the run. And it's a shame because the thing I really wanted to do was the hike itself.

This is the challenge most of us and our teams face. In a workplace buzzing with distractions, finding effective and realistic ways to prioritize has never been more vital.

So how do we choose *what* to work on when we have *too much* to work on? Delineation and delegation.

DELINEATION

Delineation is more than just prioritization. It's the allocation of time plus the ability to sort masses of data into ordered and actionable information. *It's a plan of attack*. We need to move from the traditional to-do list to structured prioritization based on the needs of the particular day.

First, identify your need. I have absorbed countless books and workshops on unique and sometimes contradictory task-management systems. But they all agree on one thing: Take a few minutes at the start of the day to plan. This is not just a classic problem of productivity; it's a distinct challenge of our times. The volume of information demanding our attention has a hidden consequence: We lose the ability to differentiate between what's important and what's not. As Texas billionaire T. Boone Pickens tweeted, "When you are hunting elephants, don't get distracted chasing rabbits." The problem is everything feels like an elephant when it's all running straight for us.

Literally, just a few minutes each day can save you hours. Don't sit down and ask yourself, "What would be easy to do?" or "What would take a lot of items off my list?" Ask instead, "What do I really need to accomplish today?"

The lists I make don't assign equal value to every item. I organize *what* to work on *when*, placing tasks in one of four categories: diamonds, dollars, dirt, and dimes.

Diamonds

The most mentally arduous tasks—diamonds—remind us why it's called *work*. But these items determine the success of my day. When I finish them, my sense of accomplishment soars because I've put a deposit on my future. These tasks are, therefore, as valuable as diamonds.

Usually, I schedule only a few of them, rarely more than three or four. It's okay to have just one (like I did today).

The key is to never assign a task you can't finish in one day. If it's too big for that, shrink the scope. Instead of "write a book," the task becomes "write Chapter 18." As a side note, I do have a place where I list out major work for the week. I call that dynamite because it makes a major impact and you can't ignore it for long without serious consequences. Most of your daily diamonds will come from this list.

Always schedule diamonds for your most attentive time of the day. As we talked about in Chapter 6, this is the morning for the vast majority of us, though there are a precious few who do exceptional work further into the day while the rest of us long for our preschool nap mats. Also keep in mind our discussion in Chapter 6 about the importance of food and rest—you want to tackle your diamonds at your peak level of performance.

Dollars

I can do dollars on autopilot. Picking up laundry, sending a deadline reminder to my team, replying to simple e-mails. These tasks need to be done but don't require significant time or attention.

Dollars aren't super-valuable on their own, but they become valuable when multiplied. So that's how you should attack them—in bunches. Take a break from your mentally taxing diamond and churn out 10 dollars.

Dirt

It might seem odd, but this is the heart of the list. These are the items I let myself ignore . . . for now.

In the constantly connected workplace, we simply can't get to every task. It's like dirt—everywhere and impossible to remove completely.

People typically never create this list because it feels counterintuitive. Why write down something you won't do now? Here's why: Disengagement grows when people don't feel like they're getting work done; better to give up and watch cat videos.

Instead of giving up, label the task dirt. Yes, intentionally remove tasks that others want you to do when doing them would make you less effective.

For leaders, dirt opens the door to conversations about tasks your people aren't finishing. Ultimately, this will help everyone readjust priorities.

You can revisit these tasks when you have time. Dirt might even become diamonds next week, but for now, actual diamonds, as well as dollars, need your attention. By labeling tasks dirt, you clear space in your mind.

When it comes to your dirt list, keep these three things in mind:

1. It's not a list of "never going to do these." If it were that, it would just get deleted from the list.

2. If you execute your day perfectly, your dirt list becomes the starting point for your next day's list.

3. Any task you think you need to do gets automatically assigned to dirt because it's your ongoing list of future to-dos. Then move it to dollars or diamonds should it need to be done that day.

And don't worry: Great ideas will eventually glitter no matter what you call them now. Your dirt, if it's worth listing on your to-do list, will always eventually become a dollar or a diamond.

Dimes

I take the label for this secondary category from a friend whose grandfather did the dime-behind-the-ear trick. Dimes, then, are little surprises or treats.

A task becomes a dime when it's more fun or interesting than important. Maybe an article shared by a colleague or a LinkedIn seminar on creative writing. Dimes provide breaks and might even help professional development. But they're not urgent.

Here's an example of my to-do list I made using these categories (Figure 18.1).

DELEGATION

I have a client who excelled at leading the largest annual fundraiser for a successful nonprofit. But she had to squeeze in the work because her boss delegated urgent tasks every day.

"I need a chart for the meeting this afternoon."

"Call the national office and see what's holding up the funding."

Everything was a fire that he seemed to trust only her to put out. The problem was that she essentially became the highest paid executive assistant in the organization. This goes to show that there is a right way and a wrong way to delegate tasks.

Some tasks do need to be on someone else's to-do list. Delegation doesn't just lighten your load; it gives your team a chance to grow and learn. I've met far too many leaders who try to do everything themselves, taking pride in working 14-hour days. Their work suffers.

I've also seen the opposite. Despite conventional leadership gurus saying otherwise, the top concern today isn't that type A leaders don't delegate enough. It's that these leaders waste their people's resources asking for things they could get themselves through, say, a simple search. (Your employees aren't Siri, so why would you ask them what year Facebook went public?)

Dynamite — *this week's goal(s)*

Diamonds — *today's priority tasks*

Dollars — *straightforward, combinable tasks*

●●● 3 MORE ITEMS

Dirt — *ignore for now*

●●● 14 MORE ITEMS

Dimes — *unimportant but fun/interesting*

10¢

Figure 18.1　D's Delineation Guide.

Leaders with this mindset ask for what's easy without considering the tasks their employees *won't* be doing as a result. Everything has a cost, even if you don't see it or feel it immediately.

Even worse, many leaders provide no context or clear picture for how their requests connect to frontline goals. So, the team jumps in without the ability to accurately adjust workloads.

These employees would love to work on their diamonds and ignore the dirt. The trouble is they don't know how and lack the information to differentiate between the two.

If delegating is easy for you, it's probably hard on your team. Before handing off a task, consider workload and whether your request is the best use of your team's resources and talents. It is helpful to consider your employees' attention resources in aggregate. Rather than simply thinking that delegating something will save you time, realize that you are paying everyone on your team for their attention and you are the steward of those resources. Just like switching tasks costs you time, there is a cost to delegation. It doesn't mean you shouldn't delegate; it just means you must be aware of whether you are doing a bad transaction for your own attention bank account.

For this reason, it's very helpful to designate the tasks you are delegating as either diamonds, dollars, or dirt or dimes. By doing so, you can prioritize what you'll pass along and what you won't, and you'll help your team know what is most important for them to spend their time and energy on.

TAKE A MINUTE

What does all of this look like for you today?

Before starting the next chapter, take a piece of paper and make a task list for today (or tomorrow if it's nighttime). What are your diamonds, dollars, dirt, and dimes? Anything need to be delegated?

What's the one task that, if finished, would make you feel amazing? When is the best time to do it?

Encourage your team to make their own lists and ask the same questions.

CHAPTER **19**

Can We Get an Extension?

I don't hate all birds. Just the one that chirps relentlessly outside my window each morning at 6 AM. My dog, on the other hand, indiscriminately chases every bird, except the one I wish he would.

One morning, that bird cost me more than just sleep. It deprived me of the focus I needed to write a blog, an article, and a speech—tasks I had blocked out on my morning calendar. I was so tired that I simply couldn't get them done well.

As leaders, we don't need any help losing sleep. A survey in the *Harvard Business Review* found that 43 percent of us feel sleep-deprived at least four nights a week.[1] This makes not only the end of the day a total loss but even the middle of the day a serious battle, no matter how much we have to get done. Marathoners expect to hit the wall at mile 20. If they are hitting it at mile 8, they have a problem.

As we learned in Chapter 6, our ability to focus is a limited commodity. Like any commodity, our success is dictated by how well we allocate it. But how do we do that well? Let's look at some simple ways to maximize focus expenditures for ourselves and our people.

Cut Bad Expenses

How many choices did you make this morning before even stepping into work?

- Should I get up now or hit snooze? Snooze.
- Which shirt would look best? The one that's least wrinkled.
- Which coffee should I brew? Screw it; I'll stop at Starbucks.

- Eat a big breakfast or something on the run? Depends. Can I con my partner into cooking?

- Should I post on Facebook? Um, of course.

One of the best ways to cut our focus expenses is to automate mornings and reduce choices. This begins the night before.

I pick out my outfit for the next day and lay it out. After setting the alarm, I choose coffee and set the timer to brew it as I get up. My wife and I discuss breakfast (we try to eat together in the morning).

Then I do my first round of prioritization, calendar open, organizing diamonds and dollars and moving some items to dirt.

Now my morning won't be cluttered with decisions. Every choice we're compelled to make complicates our ability to choose right the next time.

But morning is just the first battleground. According to *The Art of Choosing*, we average about 70 choices a day. CEOs average 139 daily tasks.[2] The more we can automate and reduce these choices, the more we reserve our precious attention resources for the ones that matter.

Our choices are like RAM in an old computer. After the computer runs for a while, it slows down. The more programs you open, the more it chugs—until you need a reboot.

The fewer programs we access in our brains, the more RAM is available for the work we need to do.

This also holds true on an organizational level. Michael Mankins of Bain & Company says the typical company loses more than a quarter of its productivity to organizational drag—procedures that waste time and stymie accomplishment.[3] The *Harvard Business Review* reports that it costs the economy more than $3 trillion a year in lost productivity.[4]

Often the easiest solution to a problem is to create a blanket policy and an extra layer of risk protection. We feel the pain from not having the policy but neglect the hidden cost of life with it. I worked at a company that protected themselves contractually from the rare worst-case-scenario and would walk away from clients who wouldn't agree to their terms. The loss in business and time assuredly added up to several times the risk they were hedging against.

The truth is organizations of any size can eliminate red tape. For instance, Netflix allows every employee to sign their own vendor contracts and lacks an expense policy, instead trusting employees to act in the company's best interests. The rationale: Letting employees use their best judgment will ultimately make them more productive.

But sometimes a lack of rules can sap our focus accounts by presenting even more choices. Should I expense a lunch where we spent, at best, two minutes discussing an account? Should I book a three-star or four-star hotel?

Netflix aside, scant boundaries can foster a culture where everyone feels compelled to work all the time. As leaders, sometimes we need to set limits that relieve them of that choice. And many other ones.

Take task scheduling. An employee's own method might actually work better. But now she must spend time and focus deciding which tasks to do instead of following a schedule that decides for her.[5]

Decentralizing any kind of decision making runs this risk. A department-store chain may let local managers decide on pricing, loss leaders, and social media, tapping into regional expertise. But having to make these choices keeps managers from focusing on other important tasks.

If you take away certain tasks and responsibilities, some of your folks might get their hackles up. No one likes the feeling of losing autonomy, even if it's best for them and the organization. One of the ways you can avoid resistance to healthy barriers and rules is to put it in the context of freeing their resources for more important decisions and tasks. Of course, that means you actually have to give them these.

The goal, on both an individual and organizational level, is to bank as much of our attention resources as possible.

Spend Them Wisely

Managing attention resources means shrewd spending, not more. Longer workweeks don't boost the bottom line. A Stanford study revealed that productivity drops sharply when people work more than 50 hours.[6] Anything past 55 hours is practically pointless.

One of the best ways to spend our focus well is by planning our day from hardest to easiest, allowing for uninterrupted chunks of time.

Tony Schwartz, president and CEO of The Energy Project, echoes this advice. "Manage your energy, not your time," he preaches, arguing that our minds can typically focus on a given task for only 90 to 120 minutes.[7] After that, we need a 20- to 30-minute break to recharge. When we ignore these blocks and breaks, we might keep moving forward, but the quality of our work decreases significantly. If you are pushing past your focus time without recharging, you're losing productivity whether you know it or not.

And the most important recharge starts before your day does.

Take Five

Neuroscientist Sandra Bond Chapman has a deceptively simple way to rest the brain for high performance. Take five 5-minute breaks each day away from technology and work.[8] Chapman suggests scheduling these breaks or setting a timer to ring every 1.5 hours or so to remind you to take one.

Even a bathroom break can yield a breakthrough. "It really is just because they stopped trying (to) push through," Chapman told *Fast Company*. "The brain break is one of the ways to keep your brain's mental energy on high charge."

Watch Something Funny...Seriously

When volunteers are paid modestly for each simple mathematical task they perform over and over, they do about 10 percent more work after watching just a few minutes of a comedy show.

Why is this? When we are in a more positive emotional state, we are more willing to delay immediate gratification. When we are in a negative emotional state, we will do whatever we can to fix the immediate problem. Sometimes pushing through is just slowing you down and delaying the inevitable.

As a side note, a boring video or something otherwise not uplifting lacks the same benefit. To save you the trouble, here are some videos I recommend (just search for the titles on YouTube):

- *America's Funniest Home Videos* compilations (if my wife is giggling uncontrollably while looking at her phone, she's watching one of these)

- Kids coming off anesthesia (the classic "David After Dentist")

- "Charlie Bit My Finger" (funny no matter how old)

- Anything by Dude Perfect (a fellow Texas A&M University Aggie—Gig 'em)

Park It

But don't just run down to the corner for a bagel. Find a park or other natural setting for your walk.

A group of psychologists divided exhausted workers into two groups.[9] Group A took a short stroll through a busy downtown. Group B walked through a natural environment such as a park.

Although the first group didn't perform any better back at work, the second one focused much better on key tasks. It's called attention restoration theory, and even looking at nature photos can do the trick.

For your next one-on-one or otherwise small meeting, try walking to a park instead of the conference room. Some people open up more when side by side with another person. And the movement will boost attention.

Put in the Hours

The best deposit you can make in your attention resources account is rest. That starts with a good night's sleep, which requires truly disconnecting.

Smartphones are far from a lullaby or glass of warm milk. They keep us mentally chained to work and make it harder to shed the cares of the day so we can unwind and get the rest we need to operate at our best.

Late-night phone use, including e-mail, renders employees more tired and less engaged at the office (reminder from Chapter 17: If they are always available, they are never fully available). As leaders, we can help by not e-mailing at night (it's easy enough to schedule morning delivery). But we should also build a culture that frees our employees to enjoy their evenings unless something comes up that is absolutely necessary.

P.S. You should also rethink leaving your phone next to the bed. You can't check e-mail—or send one—when it's out of reach.

P.P.S. Full disclosure: I sleep with my phone. I check it when I can't sleep. This might have been a self-reminder. I suppose we are all a work in progress, aren't we?

Section 6 offered guidance, for you and your people, about separating life and work, delineating and delegating, and spending attention resources wisely. In the final section, we'll define what focus-wise leadership means.

NOW THAT I HAVE YOUR ATTENTION . . .

For Section 6 reflection questions, summary video, and next step resources, please visit focuswise.com/book

FOCUS-WISE LEADERSHIP

CHAPTER 20

The First Filter

T here was a time in my career when I found myself surrendering my focus to what others told me, to whatever seemed new and exciting, or to whatever I was doing most recently. The challenges of the early days of starting a business left me with a poverty mindset. Anytime someone asked if we could do something, the answer was, "Yes!"—as long they would pay for it, even if it was way outside of our core competencies. I was drawn to every new possibility until one day I woke up and had seven different business units with none of them properly staffed or funded. Eventually, my chief operating officer, Paul, sat me down and said something I'll never forget: "My fear for you isn't that you won't have success. It's that you will look up and realize that the organization you created isn't what you actually wanted."

I knew Paul was right. I had misdirected my focus. Worse, I hadn't directed it all. "What should we do?" I asked Paul. He said, "We need a first filter."

A first filter is a guiding question that we can put every idea, possibility, dream, and strategy through to determine whether it will move us in the right direction or misdirect our focus.

That year, our first filter became: Is it driving revenue in the business we want to grow? To arrive at that filter, we forced ourselves to answer four key questions.

Question 1: What Do We Want?

In *Alice in Wonderland*, the Cheshire Cat asks, "Where do you want to go?"

"I don't know," Alice replies.

The cat says, "Then it doesn't matter which path you take."

If we don't know what we want, we won't ever get it.

As Ryan Holiday, the bestselling author of *Ego Is the Enemy* and *The Obstacle Is the Way*, wrote "This is a fundamental irony of most people's lives. They don't quite know what they want to do with their lives. Yet they are very active."[1]

If you know what you want, you will selectively attend to the opportunities throughout all of life that take you in that direction. The friend of a friend you just met can offer strategic insight and connections rather than simply casual conversation. The podcast you have teed up for the commute home can speak into overcoming a recent obstacle rather than simply help you avoid the silence.

This dynamic of selective attention has a bigger impact than even the active choices we make to move our career forward. It dictates what our eyes see, our ears hear, our minds process at any moment given the nearly infinite options available. It's much like what happens after we buy a car. Prior to the purchase, we believe the car to be rare. After purchase, we find them everywhere.

We subconsciously subvert the question of what we want by changing it to "What am I supposed to want?" or "What's the newest, shiniest trend?" Asking ourselves what we *really* desire is scary and dangerous—yet absolutely critical.

If it's ultimately a bad goal, the only way to change it is to expose it. More likely, it's a great goal that you've ignored amid the noise of everyone else's opinions. Either way, honestly asking the question is the only way for leaders to steer a course through distractions.

Let me be clear: This is first a personal question. Yes, what your organization wants is part of it, but we can't start there.

I have a friend who was brilliant, hardworking, and on track to be a managing partner at his firm. But he didn't want a huge salary and a company car; he wanted to be a dad and have more time with his family.

Now he's the best admin I've ever met—all because he asked himself the right question.

As a leader, you are also tasked with asking the plural version of this question. "What does my team want? What does my organization want?"

It's often dangerous in business to ask your employees what they really want. They might say, "I want to be the boss." But what makes this question so powerful when you honestly ask it of your team is that it gives them the chance to really consider it. Often, you can prevent them from leaving by simply knowing what they really want. You can help them see how what they are doing now can get them where they want to be, and you can be honest about what they have to change to have any shot.

Question 2: What Do They Need?

This is the more operational question. "They" are the ones you report to—boss, upper management, customer—and those who report to us.

What does our team need to succeed? Are we equipping or distracting them?

What do those above us need? As leaders, we need to filter the answer through our own wisdom and experience. Not everything the boss throws at us is useful, and it's our job to communicate and prioritize.

What does our customer need? An Uber driver who picked me up from the airport failed to properly ask this question.

He had shelled out $10,000 for a backseat karaoke system, complete with a screen, microphone, and elaborate lighting. It was massively impressive—and irrelevant. Uber customers want fast-and-easy transportation. Even 24-hour party people will choose a driver based on proximity rather than fun.

If you are considering whether to grow, start, or shut down a product or business line, it is key to ask, "What do they need? Is there a real demand for this?"

My staff is well-versed and highly efficient in the back-office functions required for my busy speaking calendar. We added a business line to help other speakers with similar services. Unfortunately, most of the people who kept approaching us really just needed sales. They weren't getting booked to speak yet. Thus, they didn't need back-office support.

It's crucial to break down and then focus on the elements of what the customer needs. I've seen companies waste millions of dollars on things that aren't part of the buying decision. Buy-in usually results from just a small number of factors.

We need to give customers what they want—and most often, not more than that.

Question 3: What Can We Do?

The short answer: not as much as we might like. I know. Some of us like to think we can do everything better than everyone else.

A friend shared the story of a time he spoke at a speaker showcase, an event where a speaker bureau hosts a number of event planners at a single venue to review several speakers live. After my friend's speech, he was approached by a well-known speaker whose per event honorarium is $35,000. The speaking legend said, "Awesome speech! When I heard it, I thought you must be a $15K speaker. Then I noticed you spoke on another topic, so I dropped your fee down to $10K. Then I noticed yet another topic. Down to $5K. Another—you were now free. And another—you now owe me $5K to listen to you talk about anything." The lesson wasn't lost on my friend, a then up-and-coming speaker. If you try to know or do everything, you will not be worth much of anything to anyone.

A simple litmus test: If you think something will be simple and easy, you don't understand what it will take and what it will cost. And you shouldn't do it.

The key is to do what we do well and let others do what they do well.

Being a focus-wise leader means understanding not just where focus belongs but also when. In his book, *To Explain the World: The Discovery of Modern Science*, Steven Weinberg wrote, "An essential feature of scientific progress [is] to understand which problems are ripe for study and which are not."[2]

He goes on to tell the story of two leading physicists at the beginning of the twentieth century, Hendrik Lorentz and Max Abraham. They devoted themselves to understanding the recently discovered electron but to no avail. Why? They were missing a key to understanding: quantum physics, which wasn't discovered until two decades later.

These brilliant men spent all their time and energy chasing something that it wasn't time for. Another brilliant man chose a different path. As Weinberg writes, "The development of the special theory of relativity by Albert Einstein was made possible by Einstein's refusal to worry about what electrons were. Instead he worried about how observations of anything (including electrons) depend on the motion of the observer."[3]

Albert Einstein didn't develop the theory of relativity by chasing the just-discovered electron as his contemporaries did early in the twentieth century. He focused on what could be solved *now*, leaving quantum mechanics to address the nature of electrons two decades later.

Einstein was focus-wise, but it doesn't take a genius to follow his example.

Timing truly is everything. Knowing when to jump in—instead of, for instance, pursuing an initiative just because it's new—is key to our first filter.

Do we devote energy to tasks that can't be done without additional information (like Einstein's fellow physicists) or that are otherwise beyond our control? Do we make useless comparisons to our own work?

Question 4: What's Keeping What I Want, What They Need, and What I Can Do from Happening at the Level It Could?

It's always been difficult to discern when to say no, what to stop doing, and when to pull back in order to refocus. But today, it's harder than ever.

I consulted for a major nonprofit that prided itself on nurturing new ideas. Every week, employees were encouraged to share them.

As a result, the organization was perpetually changing process and shifting roles. They thought innovation meant constant change, but that constant change stymied innovation. Great ideas never had a chance to take root and flourish. The result was simply chaos.

We love the new. It's alluring. Endless possibilities exist in the not-yet-known or accomplished. We even have a word for the seductiveness of novelty: *neophilia*.

In truth, we don't need new ideas every week. We need people to execute the things we already know we're supposed to do. Technology, however, stokes the fires of neophilia. Every new smartphone, OS, and content management system calls to us like the Sirens from Chapter 2. It's FOMO (fear of missing out) on steroids.

Just as our infatuation with the new can be damaging to our call to set the right strategy and direction, so too can becoming so fixated on small details that we can't see the bigger picture.

In a now classic experiment at Harvard, subjects were asked to watch a video and count the number of times people passed a basketball. Half of the viewers missed something peculiar: a gorilla walking through the scene.[4]

"This experiment reveals two things: that we are missing a lot of what goes on around us, and that we have no idea that we are missing so much," researchers Christopher Chabris and Daniel Simons wrote.

Or to put it another way, you can be focused without being focus-wise.

I once fired someone for being too meticulous. Despite my efforts to keep him focused on the larger goal of his task, he became so distracted by small details that he couldn't reach the finish line. If I'd asked him to mop a kitchen floor, he probably would have spent all day on a 3-inch patch of grout.

We can't be so focused on what's right in front of us that we miss important factors around us. We have to see the forest *and* the trees.

That's also what happens with the HiPPO (highest paid person's opinion). Lacking context on a project or issue, an executive or VP will stir things up, steal focus, and redirect it to things that don't matter.

But just because parking space assignments anger him doesn't mean everyone should focus on redesigning the parking lot.

APPLYING THE FIRST FILTER

Intel had thrived in the memory chip business since 1968 but, by the mid-1980s, had to ponder a new identity. Seeing the trends in low-cost competition, Intel made a huge bet on microprocessors. The result is that you can probably hear the "Intel Inside" jingle in your head right now. Companies like Intel, which have thrived in a highly competitive industry for decades, continually run their decisions through first filters.

The first filter helps make all of the decisions needed to move forward successfully easier. In a world filled with distractions, we as leaders need this first filter to gauge what we want, what's needed, and what we can do in pursuit of our goals. Because when you arrive at the sweet spot where those three things meet, you have your strategy.

Going back to our to-do list method of diamonds, dollars, and dirt, your diamonds are much easier to identify from your dirt when you have absolute clarity on your strategic direction—and that comes from applying the first filter. When we use it, everything else falls right into place. Focus only serves us if it's trained on the right things.

I've witnessed the power of these questions in my own company. Our aim is to help people create real change in the way they approach work in a world of constant connectivity. We accomplish this by giving people what they need, namely tools to help them at every level of engagement, from simple worksheets to this book you're reading to videos, support networks, a helpful speech, practical trainings, and more. This caused us to take a serious look at what we could do. I chose to focus on one unified brand rather than dividing my team, assets, leadership, and attention resources. This caused the focus we needed for me to both produce and manage the business—increasing revenue in the process. That's the power of the four questions that form the first filter.

This filter set the course for all our actions. Every question of what we should or shouldn't do was therefore matched against the larger question of whether it drove revenue. Our success amazed me, and it came from training all our focus on key areas instead of whatever someone else imposed on us.

The first filter is something that should adorn every hat we wear in life. At home, my wife and I use our first filter—is this decision contributing to loving one another and spending time together?—for every decision that matters.

Now, this doesn't mean you will never make a single decision that falls outside of the first filter. I go on a trip to Colorado to fly fish every year. That doesn't get me more time with my family, but by having that filter set up, it ensures I am intentional about the times I am gone.

My friend Thomas Kim, an entrepreneur, describes the power of the first filter in this way: "Just because I can, doesn't mean I should. Just because it's new and exciting, doesn't make it deeply fulfilling. Just because I have the opportunity, doesn't make it God's bidding. A growth opportunity in some ways can stunt my growth in others. When I say 'yes' to this, I'm also saying 'no' to something else. When I say 'no' to this, I'm saying 'yes' to things I'm already doing."

Do you have a first filter to help steer your focus? Take some time and jot down answers to the four core questions from this chapter.

CHAPTER 21

Individual to Institutional

A friend of mine who works at a large tech company describes a romance familiar to many of us.

A new employee, aglow from the courtship of recruitment and multiple interviews, can't wait to start the relationship. The company culture is exactly what he's been seeking. "Energized" doesn't begin to describe how he feels about his new role and its place in the organization.

The honeymoon ends abruptly. Faced with bureaucracy, politics, and inertia, the employee soon realizes that he faces three options:

- Become a zombie who ignores his instincts and makes decisions based on ease and convenience instead of what best serves the company

- Buy into the nonsense, becoming ultra-competitive and political while ignoring the actual work and his own professional growth

- File for divorce (i.e., quit)

None of these options bodes well for future work relationships.

Culture is the internal script that shapes behavior and expectations in a workplace. It determines what's appropriate and what's not, what's laughable and what's fireable. For example, drinking too much at the holiday party will get you a promotion at one place (been there) and fired at another (friend whose been there). Put aside rafts and sailboats for a moment: Culture has the turning radius of an aircraft carrier and a very small rudder. Changing course can be extremely difficult.

Great ideas can quickly drown in the chop of this ship, even when they would benefit everyone.

One of my clients desperately pushed for improvements at his company, fully aware that resistance often accompanies change. A new project-management system was installed, freeing PMs to think and act instead of simply following orders lobbed over by executives.

That's the dream, right?

Alas, it didn't happen in this case. A logical, liberating new system ran smack into the wall of command-and-control change leadership. It was part of a culture that:

- Stunts employee engagement and commitment, often fostering resistance

- Reduces the chance of enacting change that will lead to success

- Prevents leaders from making vital course corrections during implementation

- Downplays attention to consistent communication and emotional reaction to change[1]

The buck stops at culture.

We must create a culture that supports the goal of become focuswise. As leaders, we need to move from individually valuing focus to reinforcing the broader message of it. So how do we actually create an environment that removes us from the hamster wheel of constant connectivity?

CHANGE AS A VALUE

It cannot be emphasized enough: Having a culture that values change and agility is crucial. This is not the neophiliac organization so addicted to what it *isn't* that it never grasps what it is. More than any other time in history, today's organizations need to be sailboats, flexible and adaptive to the moments and contexts surrounding them.

Historically, the largest organizations have thrived by enshrining the status quo. That was before the constantly connected workplace. Today—with the needs of the customer perpetually shifting and evolving, demanding that skillsets expand to accommodate them—organizations simply must foster a culture that values fluidity.

So how can we ensure that this sleek new Ferrari of a culture has the focus-wise chassis to match?

Introduce the Need for Change

In the now famous monologue from *Glengarry Glen Ross*, a successful sales consultant (Alec Baldwin) gets up in front of four struggling real estate salesmen and introduces himself by saying, "The good news is you're fired. The bad news is you've got—all of you got—just one week to regain your jobs, starting with tonight." The rest of the profanity-laced speech is the consultant telling the salesmen how horrible they are. Needless to say, he doesn't endear himself to the salesmen.

Although change has to start with an introduction, how you do it can make all the difference. Tough sales speeches make great cinema, but they rarely make great teams. It's amazing how many great ideas get lost solely on the poor people skills of the person introducing the change.

It starts by introducing the need for it to your people. Because why would anyone want to change something if he doesn't understand why it needs to be changed?

One of the best ways to introduce change is by motivating the problem. *Motivating*, in this sense, means exposing the need. Our people need to truly believe something is wrong before we can propose a solution.

Steve Jobs did this famously in a speech detailing everything wrong with current phones before unveiling the iPhone as the solution to the problem in 2007. Communications guru Nancy Duarte calls this a "two-worlds approach"—how the world is and how the world could be (that is, much better).

Introducing the need to be focus-wise in our workplaces begins by motivating the problem. Something's wrong with how work is done. You can flip back to the earliest chapters in this book and identify numerous examples that will resonate with your people and help them recognize the urgency of the problem—and that becoming focus-wise is the solution.

How you frame the problem and solution for your people is everything. Know when to make it about them and when to make it about you.

Make it about them by framing the entire situation around helping them. Make it about you by saying, "I have a problem too." Remember: You're not the hero fixing everything your team is doing wrong—that's a recipe for resistance. *All* of you are the heroes, fixing what ails your organization.

Another strategy is to find someone from the outside to introduce it. When you bring in an "expert" to launch the conversation with a great speech, you avoid being the bad guy and you get everyone excited and on the same page.

Framing the problem also means injecting a cool factor. It's called priming. Find apps and connections that your people are already primed to like.

Broccoli is nutritious, but it isn't cool. That's why a training session should never be offered as the remedy for your team's terrible diet. It should be touted as a delicacy that Anthony Bourdain would go halfway around the world to eat:

Guess what we're getting? That amazing new productivity app Inc. *magazine and CNET can't stop raving about.*

Include Your People in the Decision Making

The psychology is undeniable. It doesn't matter how much they need change. It doesn't matter how much they yearn for it. If they aren't given the chance to shape the process, they'll resist it.

Why?

As Dean Anderson and Linda Ackerman Anderson point out, "Employees frequently receive critical data for course correction long before leaders because employees are closer to the action. They are key to the early warning system for needed adjustments to both the goals of the transformation and the plans for getting there."[2]

Your employees most likely know the problems your organization is facing better than you do. And they know that if they don't get a chance to own the solution, the problems will most likely never get solved.

After you introduce the concept, start a discussion and elicit their feedback. What works? What's causing problems? What can be done to fix them? Getting your people involved will give you a lot more leeway down the road.

This is where the Communication Compact we introduced in Chapter 14 becomes even more important. Your team will already have the template for sharing information in a way that makes them feel valued and heard.

Equip Your People with the Tools to Succeed

If you're establishing vault time, give everyone a sign or a pair of headphones. How about a guide to apps that help block out distractions or a link with a quick how-to about turning off push notifications?

It's amazing how often we target a desired behavior without offering the resources critical to making it happen. You can't expect your team to find their own tools.

Also, how you equip them matters. Your employees have limited attention resources. So every hoop you make them jump through to make the change increases the likelihood they won't do it. Rather than sending a four-page document with several steps, create a short video that walks them through setting up filters for who can reach them when.

Reinforce the Culture Again and Again

Although well-intentioned, we are creatures of habit (remember one of the four hidden factors from Chapter 6: experience). You're asking people to take a harder road rather than walking along the same neural paths they've known for years.

If you want them to stop e-mailing every time they have a question, what are some creative ways to reinforce the reminder? Signs posted everywhere. Check-ins during meetings to see how the group is doing.

Brendon Maxwell, founder of Utopian Coffee, reinforced the company's culture of service by posting a huge picture board of the people that his own people had helped. No one walking in the door can miss it.

How you act matters; so does what you say and how you say it. Use focus-wise language, for instance, to create verbal reminders to back up your focus-wise actions.

Finally, choose one thing to reinforce over a sustained period of time. I often see organizations hire people like me to help on an issue, but unfortunately, they don't reinforce the message beyond that day. Even worse, they bring in several totally different messages on the same day. In our desire to cram in content, we forget that the point of good content is to actually act on it. Consider bringing back the same person to speak on the same topic multiple times, or follow the speaker with a webinar, online training, and a check-in call.

Incentivize the Right Behaviors

"Show me the incentive and I will show you the outcome."
Charlie Munger, Warren Buffet's legendary business partner

Incentive is one of the most important tools for a leader. Are you rewarding the right behaviors or the wrong ones?

It continually astonishes me how often organizations say they want one thing then reward the opposite. Don't incentivize e-mail volume by encouraging those who e-mail at all hours of the night. Reward someone for *not* answering an e-mail on vacation. Make sure your reward system reflects your focus-wise approach.

One of my clients, Eric Maddox, is the most successful interrogator in the history of the U.S. military. He's the person responsible for finding Saddam Hussein. However, when Eric entered the military, he saw that interrogations had an atrocious success rate. He resolved to find out why.

While stationed in Iraq, he accompanied the special ops team on their missions to conduct field research into interrogations. His findings told him that by the time he saw people for interrogations back at the safety of his base, the game was already lost.

So he changed the rules and started traveling with the special ops team regularly. Why would he put himself in such a dangerous situation when he could just wait until they got back? Because he knew if he could interrogate someone in their own home, he had a much better chance of understanding motivation and aligning incentives accordingly.

He could assure them with what amounted to a reward: "If you give me this information, we will leave and you can stay home with your family."

Military interrogation may seem like a stark analogy for your organization. But what matters is the psychology, which translates to any situation. Incentives reward desired behavior.

That being said, incentives can be pleasurable and fun. Be creative; even include your team in the process. Let the group set the consequences.

If you're on the phone during a meeting, you have to clean the whiteboard in the conference room.

If you send an e-mail after 9 p.m., you have to bring that person breakfast.

Interrupt someone in her vault, and you owe her Starbucks.

But also foster a culture in which the wrong person can be removed from a team. Corporate America fails consistently in this regard, hamstrung by its own policies.

I worked with a prominent tech company that struggled with a person dragging the team down. Removing him wasn't just a matter of taking him to coffee and saying, "We need to talk." The manager had to repeatedly document the problem, put the employee on probation, and slot him into a coaching program.

The title character in Herman Melville's classic short story "Bartleby, the Scrivener: A Story of Wall Street" gradually refuses to work, driving his boss mad by repeating, "I would prefer not to." My client's problem employee could have been Bartleby's cousin. He literally quit working, testing how long the company would keep paying him.

The strategy worked. He drew his salary for a year before being let go—with severance. No one at the company could provide an incentive—or disincentive—more powerful than his own.

Documenting the problem shouldn't be part of a yearlong process, but it is nonetheless vital. So is acting quickly as part of a hire-slow/fire-fast philosophy. As leaders, we need to have the important conversations early.

One of my clients who works for a wholesale foods provider inherited an employee from the former head of the department. Besides failing at his job, the person was caustic and aggressive with everyone in the office.

My client, an exceptional leader, confronted the employee immediately. He detailed the performance and behavior issues that would no longer be tolerated.

What the manager learned in doing so was eye-opening—and instructive: The employee had acted the same way for 5 years and was astonished at how people perceived him. Clearly, his former manager shared some blame here.

To create a focus culture, you must first be clear about what needs to change. Once you've made a true believer of yourself, the basic question gains even more focus and urgency:

Are you rewarding the right behaviors or the wrong ones?

I recently spoke for a financial services organization. Leadership sought to implement a focus-wise culture. The three-day conference was built on this theme. Every speaker and every activity reinforced the message. They didn't stop there. They issued a 30-day mindfulness challenge. Leadership then provided an app to guide the daily exercise, set reminders, and hold participants accountable. The CEO offered to donate $100,000 to charity if they got 100 percent participation. They introduced, equipped, reinforced, and incentivized this new behavior.

It takes work to plan and execute, but change can happen.

Sometimes it's a matter of proper training, as we'll learn in the next chapter.

CHAPTER 22

Filling the Digital Skill Gaps

In a perfect world, you would hire people who were perfectly prepared to do the job you needed them to do. The nature of work is constantly changing, and a combination of trends has merged to create consistent gaps in the skillsets of employees. Roles are becoming more specialized, and education (from kindergarten to college) isn't keeping up.

The CEO of Zipcar puts it succinctly: "My father had one job in his lifetime. I will have six jobs in my lifetime, and my children will have six jobs at the same time."

These splintered experiences of work have combined to create employees who are decent at a wide variety of things but not necessarily experts at even a few.

This means you have to play an active role in filling the gaps. Training people to succeed ultimately falls to you—including the how of focused work in a constantly connected workplace.

THE SKILLS TO TRAIN

Aside from focus-wise skills, what do your people need in a world of relentless connectivity? Though you may add skills specific to your own business, the two that every modern workplace requires relate to communication and technology.

Effective Communication

If you're immersed in digital all the time, your other skills will suffer. (This book is overflowing with examples.) The more time we spend staring at screens, the worse we become at face-to-face interaction.

Empathy declines because we can't see facial cues. *Is Chris angry . . . or constipated? I wish he'd text another emoji so I could figure it out!*

Digital natives find themselves at an even greater disadvantage because their brain rewiring makes them slower to pick up on nonverbal cues in normal conversation. "That could be a liability if you want to work in a field such as consulting, financial advising, and diplomacy that requires face-to-face interactions," John K. Mullen writes in the *Harvard Business Review*.[1]

Digital-first people try to handle issues through e-mail, texting, or the like—often turning conflict into conflagration (see Chapter 16, "Face to Face in a Facebook World").

Presentation skills also fall under this category. Through the ages, rhetoric has been considered one of the most important skills to master; it was one of the first three units of Aristotle's classical education. In a world filled with distraction, it's even more crucial to success. In the past, we were forced to listen to the incoherent ramblings of a CEO, but today, we all have Candy Crush to distract us.

In a world gone digital, rhetoric is no longer widely taught. Yet it's never been more crucial. In an analysis of 2.3 million LinkedIn profiles, almost 58 percent of workers who presented superior communications skills were hired in the course of a year.[2]

Companies hire people who demonstrate soft skills such as communication, teamwork, punctuality, and organization. But for some reason, they usually don't train their existing employees in these skills. That must change.

Digital Competency

The heroes of *Men in Black* battle comically huge and grotesque insects to save the world. One of their most important weapons is a pen-like device that erases people's memories, preempting dicey questions about aliens stomping around New York.

Important as the device is, Agent J (Will Smith) spends much of the movie fumbling with how to use it. (Mercifully, no one grills him about how it actually works.)

The irony of the movie stretches to this chapter. In a world saturated by technology, you might think the one area that wouldn't require training is tech use. Yet it's a significant problem.

Our immersion in all things digital doesn't necessarily make us good at it. It's become so user-friendly that we almost don't have to be proficient. Just click here, press there, and the software does everything for us.

In a bit of reverse discrimination, leaders often hire younger employees on the assumption that they're fluent in all things digital. That's simply not the case. A Canadian study even suggests that today's digital natives are more accurately described as "digital learners."[3] It argues that despite high confidence and skills, the competence of these learners may be much lower than that of their "digital teachers."

The bottom line: We can't neglect training our people to effectively use—and take control of—the digital tools necessary for their work.

How to Train These Skills

Training can easily become passive rather than proactive. That's because we tend to guide others in a way that's easiest for us rather than most effective for them. So, we add pages to an already bloated manual or just hope they can learn by reviewing all of your past work.

How we train people is the truest marker of how much we actually value their training. We must budget enough time and money to make it shine.

Effective training begins by acknowledging the limitations of our participants. Today's employees are more distracted than ever.

Many are addicted to devices that provide endless ways to entertain them. In fact, most of them can't even watch a TV show without also browsing Facebook on their phones. No wonder typical training bores them out of their minds within the first 3 minutes.

It doesn't, of course, have to be that way. Here are some tips to lift your training beyond typical.

Change the Setting

It's easy and comfortable to keep people in front of their computers. Don't. Yank folks away so you have their full attention.

As I write this, I'm preparing for a trip to Whistler for a retreat of key leaders of a bank. There's a reason organizations go on retreats. When we get away from the same environment, we are more likely to leave behind distractions—and actually retain the important information we learn.

My workshops are old-school. I strive to be dynamic at the front of the room, fortifying the training session with plenty of stories and media. Meanwhile, my captive audience sits in chairs with nothing but a handout and a pen.

The only tech in the room is whatever I choose for the presentation. I do this for a living, but not even I can compete with the YouTube video someone's friend just shared with him.

Be a Curator Rather Than a Creator

Your people are used to Netflix, YouTube, and TED Talks. If you don't communicate with humor, clarity, and relevance, they'll tune you out. Today, your people can not only feast on any form of entertainment from the best the world has to offer, but they can also literally do it *from their phones* while you're talking.

Even though I speak professionally and have spent hundreds of hours preparing, I still sprinkle in entertaining videos; fun, interactive drills; and questions that require more than yes or no, just to change things up.

So maybe you're not the most polished speaker, and it may be difficult for you to compete with the world's best entertainers coming through on an iPhone screen. The good news is you don't have to compete. Instead, leverage. As the saying goes, "If you can't beat 'em; join 'em." The Web is teeming with great resources that are cheap or free. Determine the skills you want to develop, then find the corresponding resource.

It's simple and effective to watch a 10-minute video of a great communicator and lead a discussion. People will enjoy the changeup, leading to better results.

If the message needs to come from you, you can still incorporate short, entertaining videos and funny memes that illustrate your points. The goal is to emphasize the entertainment value of the presentation. Your people are used to switching platforms and content frequently in their day-to-day. Help them by switching the mediums and formats you use to deliver information.

In that vein, don't hesitate to invite professional speakers and trainers. A colleague of mine used to give sex ed presentations for classes from middle school to college. The topic, of course, automatically captured their attention. But it was also the treat of a new face and voice imparting the wisdom.

Best of all, outside professionals confer credibility on you. Hearing an expert echo your values elevates you from nag to sage, affirming your leadership.

Keep Training Sessions Short

Less is more. Except when more is more.

Like you, your people have a lot on their plates. No one wants to spend an hour listening to something that could've taken 15 minutes. By squandering your team's time, you also squander their trust in you.

This ethos extends to all-day trainings, most of which can be done in 2 hours. Plus, long sessions are expensive. Part of building a culture of effective training includes being a good steward of company resources.

That said, the skills you want to cultivate may warrant pulling your people out of their environment so they can get a full day of focus. Or split the difference: a half-day training with ongoing reinforcement of the message.

Additionally, keep the content formats you use in your training short and varied. This is not always as easy as it sounds. As Mark Twain said, "I didn't have time to write a short letter, so I wrote a long one instead." It's much easier to play a 2-hour video than to create a dynamic presentation that is well-paced and full of short but high-impact material. But it's worth it.

As for your parts of the training between that high-impact material, keep it short, especially if public speaking isn't your strong suit.

A friend of mine knows this about himself, yet he typically rattles on for 45 to 50 minutes. Funny thing is he actually holds the audience's attention for about 15 minutes before the chorus line of nodding off begins. (Maybe if he just *stopped* after 15 minutes . . .)

Lots of reading material also tests the attention spans of your people. Heavy reading is for personal time, not work. (As a side note, please stop with the group slide read-along where you put your entire presentation in writing on the PowerPoint and then proceed to read it out loud.)

People simply don't read as often anymore (just because *Moby Dick* should be read doesn't mean it will be). More people watch the news, and even those who read it aren't really reading. A recent study found that about 60 percent of us admit to scanning headlines instead of diving into the stories themselves.[4]

Overall, it's smart to replace words with video whenever possible. As mentioned, your employees are used to, and therefore comfortable with, absorbing information on a screen with moving images.

With the landscape of work and technology constantly shifting, it's never been more important to properly train your people—on not just what to do but how to be focus-wise while doing it.

CHAPTER 23

Competing with Zuckerberg

Mark Zuckerberg makes being a leader difficult. He created a platform where everyone looks amazing all the time. And he created a company where no one seemingly has to work. Everyone sits in beanbag chairs, wears pajamas to work, takes as many vacation days as needed, and plays ping pong all day long. It's tough competing with Zuckerberg. But you must.

Heavy lifting used to be just that. Our economy once relied much more on physical labor than it does today.

Today, your heavy lifting is about competing for the time and attention of your people when there is always something better, newer, and shinier out there. One example is the chronic issue of employee engagement and how it's our job as leaders to inspire people. If we don't, they'll drag down the organization or simply leave.

DIGITAL DISCONNECT

One reason that engagement lags is the shift from physical to mental labor. Typical work today requires significantly more mental focus; most people can't just zone out and do their job. And where focus is required, distraction always threatens to upend it.

But there's an even larger component that leaders, if they're focus-wise, spend their energy cultivating. Few things drive performance like emotional engagement.

As organizations and the economy become increasingly complex, employees are often denied the emotional benefit of seeing their labor bear fruit. People crave the excitement of experiencing a customer using their product or seeing a community helped by their services. But many of us work on only a tiny piece of a large whole. We're several steps removed from witnessing the difference we make.

Technology also distorts our people's perception of human experience, sapping their emotional energy. Social media paints a skewed picture in which friends and family live perfect, pain-free lives. Because that's what people post: a must-try drink at Starbucks, a postcard sunset from a beachside hotel, an anniversary picture in France. I'm sorry, but no Instagram filter is going to make your Lean Cuisine look like a five-star meal. That's all in your head.

As leaders, we're also competing with the image of companies like Facebook and Google. Fun at their offices is apparently compulsory, with employees doing little work between team-building games and giant-beanbag brainstorms. All while making stacks of cash.

Employees have never been exposed to more carefully crafted false narratives romanticizing all the things their jobs *aren't* letting them do. And they're so overwhelmed that they have less space to process and consider the purpose of their work.

Can we blame them for being emotionally disengaged?

ANALOG LEADERSHIP

To keep our people engaged, we must respond to the digital onslaught with *analog leadership*. That term—which I learned from a four-star general—refers to actively listening and intentionally connecting face to face. In a world of constant change from digital, what your people need most is to experience you in analog form. During my time working with military leadership, I witnessed firsthand how this general's approach filtered through the 400,000 people he leads as the head of this massive (though often unknown) branch of the military.

Ironically, the top-down hierarchy, often associated with the military, that dominated much of the twentieth-century corporation didn't pay much heed to inspiring employees. "A paycheck is motivation enough," you can almost hear a boss growl as he chews on a cigar. Maybe it's time for the twentieth-century corporation to learn from twenty-first-century military leadership.

This doesn't work in our digital world. You can't rely on software to expedite this part of your leadership duties. It's like vinyl records. The reason they refuse to go away, despite the scratching, popping, and hissing, is that no one has figured out how to replicate their warmth in a digital format.

Records, unlike MP3s, require cleaning, polishing, and proper storage—all "in-person" tasks. Employees require their own kind of care that must be in person.

Analog leadership is developed through practice, work, and intention. And it's absolutely indispensable to the task of inspiring your people.

A quick word on *engagement* versus *inspiration*. We've been using the terms almost interchangeably. Now let's draw a quick distinction, illustrated by Michael Mankins.

An engaged employee is 44 percent more productive than one who's merely satisfied, he tells Fast Company. But an inspired employee is 125 percent more productive.[1]

The point is that inspiration first requires engagement. And though no one can feel inspired all the time, it's still the goal.

"We've been taught that you're either a General Patton and can inspire others or you're not, but this is not true," Mankins continues. "Inspirational leadership can be taught."

So where do we start?

A Direct Link to Motivation

Guiding your people to focus wisdom will automatically increase their engagement because the importance of their work will become clear. They won't be overwhelmed by the urgent and the trivial. But effective focus on a specific task isn't enough.

Emotional engagement springs from connection. As a leader, you have to help your people bridge the gap between what they do and what they care about. I call this a direct link to an effective motivator.

Let's have a look at some potential motivators.

Job Recognition

Most people pursue a field they enjoy, and an effective leader catalyzes their strengths to accomplish productive work. But for employees, true fulfillment comes from seeing, and hearing about, the results of what they do.

Spotlight the growth in your people's work, including challenges they've overcome. Or how a project they just finished helped a colleague sign a client. Put a reminder in your calendar: "Did I make the direct link to an effective motivator this week?"

A pat on the back is even more satisfying when multiplied. Publicly celebrating someone's work guarantees he or she will see it differently.

A Shared Mission

Though "mission statements" can elicit eye rolls, having a purpose at work is the same as having one in life. Sadly, an organization's mission can be lost among layers of leadership, never energizing the people who most need to feel its impact.

Utopian Coffee is converting fields in Colombia from cocaine to coffee, bettering the lives of people in that country and far beyond. Brendon Maxwell, the company's founder, is constantly reminded of the deeper reasons behind what he does.

But he realized his staff in Fort Wayne, Indiana, wasn't seeing the full impact of Utopian's mission. So he created the huge board mentioned in Chapter 21. It connects every step in the project to photos of families whose lives are being changed.

"Sometimes on a Tuesday afternoon, the work you're doing just feels like a job, not a calling to make an impact in the world," Maxwell told me. The picture board "allows us to be more consistently connected to our bigger goals and properly aligns our cultural leaning from the moment someone walks through our door."

A True Sense of Community

Except for the dedicated Luddites among us, we all live in some sort of digital community (probably several). But as the need for analog leadership reminds us, the digital is no substitute for face-to-face community.

Neither is the automobile. As we mull the pros and cons of technology, it's easy to forget this pivotal piece of tech.

The beginning of our romance with cars signaled the cleaving of another relationship: work life from personal community. Before then, everything we did—school, commerce, church—was in some way communal. We simply didn't have the mobility to separate the spheres of our life.

What does this mean for you as a leader? It's important to remember that your team may very well lack a community outside of work. The irony of isolation is that we can feel it even when surrounded by others (including colleagues).

A shared mission is key to community, but so is fun and a general commitment to serving communities beyond work. Remember birthdays, and don't forget the cake. Schedule regular happy hours or their equivalent. Band together on a Saturday to clean up a park.

What We Create

Humans are built to work with a sense of purpose. When your folks know the end goal—the reason why their work matters—they are much more motivated to trust the entire process and deliver high-quality contributions—even if they may never see the end result.

I spoke at an aerospace and defense company and got to hear about the game-changing James Webb Space Telescope, which will study the formation of the universe and solar systems that could support life. It's set for launch in 2018.[2]

The majestic cathedrals of Europe took generations to build, requiring a buy-in from contributors who wouldn't live to see what we cherish today. The telescope offers a good analogy at scale. Far from a "fail-fast" schedule, the project began in 1996 but has kept its people energized with a sense of purpose that drives the work.

It might be a lot to ask an organization to inspire the same kind of focus and enthusiasm for two decades. But it also shouldn't be a galaxy that far, far away.

Fearless Leadership

Speaking of effective motivators, what about you?

Never underestimate the power you have to shape people's perceptions. I've watched countless CEOs and other leaders, for example, circle the wagons after making a mistake. Your people will respect you more if you're authentic with them.

Clearly there's work to do. Consider this sobering indictment: The vast majority of people do not trust the top leader of the company that employs them, according to the Edelman Trust Barometer.[3]

Kim Scott, a CEO coach and former Google executive, says leaders will vary in style, but the best of them all have one thing in common: "radical candor."[4] People will work harder for you if they see your honesty and vulnerability—something never to be confused with weakness, by the way (recall the manager who cried in Chapter 16).

Sometimes it comes down to a well-timed, well-delivered speech to elevate motivation from a wall poster at work to a way of thinking far beyond it. You don't have to be Tony Robbins (as long as you don't expect to be paid like he does for a speech) to rally the troops.

Whatever your style, try closing out each speech by letting people know how their work has affected your life. I used to think the sentiment felt canned, but I've learned that people need to hear it. And it works.

I'll leave the final word to Simon Sinek, whose famous TED Talk, "How Great Leaders Inspire Action," is a call to purpose in our work. Here's the conclusion of his speech:

> Leaders hold a position of power or authority, but those who lead inspire us. Whether they're individuals or organizations, we follow those who lead, not because we have to but because we want to. We follow those who lead, not for them but for ourselves. And it's those who start with "why" that have the ability to inspire those around them or find others who inspire them.[5]

You'd be hard-pressed to find a better definition of leadership.

CHAPTER **24**

After All, We're Here to Work

My friend Dan is a true genius. After graduating from John Hopkins University with a degree in mechanical engineering, he got what he thought would be a dream job working for a defense contractor. In reality, the only dream involved would have been the ones during the naps he could have taken at his desk because he was so bored. But rather than nap (as fulfilling as that would have been), Dan used his immense amount of free time at work to get his master's while sitting at his desk. Most folks aren't as industrious as Dan. They just watch YouTube videos . . . or actually nap.

Much of this book has been about distractions luring our people away from accomplishing focused work. In the last chapter, we exhorted you to inspire them.

Now they're leaving the pep rally and going back to work. And if their work bores them, you can be a combination of Tony Robbins, Simon Sinek, and Mark Zuckerberg, and it won't matter. They'll just become distracted again. So how do you keep your employees focused and driven when they can watch YouTube videos or take naps at their desk?

Surprisingly, the solution is simple.

Make their work harder.

It sounds counterintuitive. *My people feel overwhelmed and distracted . . . and the solution is to give them more work?*

Yes. More work, and more challenging work.

YOUR PEOPLE ARE BORED

Almost half the workforce in America is bored out of their minds. No wonder they're so easily swayed by distractions.

When asked in a survey whether their work excited them, just under half of respondents said no.[1] How would your employees answer?

At one company I worked with, half the team was watching Netflix while doing work. It was apparently the only way for them to keep awake. The sad but intriguing part is that most of them didn't want to be watching movies (even *Better Call Saul* gets boring after the sixth episode . . . before 2 PM). They just didn't feel challenged.

No one wants to browse social media all day. People want to do meaningful work. Mihaly Csikszentmihalyi speaks to this in his influential book *Flow: The Psychology of Optimal Experience*:

> Contrary to what we usually believe, moments like these, the best moments in our lives, are not the passive, receptive, relaxing times—although such experiences can also be enjoyable, if we have worked hard to attain them. The best moments usually occur when a person's body or mind is stretched to its limits in a voluntary effort to accomplish something difficult and worthwhile. Optimal experience is thus something that we make happen.[2]

Take up the challenge of providing that work. The greater the challenge, the less waste.

Paychex human resources examined which industry's workers waste the most time.[3] Construction workers, it turns out, were most likely to stay on task. In fact, 61 percent of respondents in construction said they squander less than an hour each workday. On the other hand, the results were not as kind to workers from utilities, telecom, and government sectors.

The reason is simple: they have to. The industry already faces a lack of qualified labor, tight deadlines, and constant delays.

Ah, good old-fashioned urgency. Wouldn't it be great if all workers had this kind of drive?

INCREASE YOUR EXPECTATIONS

The employees who feel overworked are actually burdened with wasteful tasks instead of the focused work that drives things forward. People fill the space they have. They complain about not having enough time because they feel busy. And they are busy—doing the wrong things.

The solution is to increase your expectations.

Teach your people new skills, then give them projects that use those skills. Eighty percent of U.S. office workers say that learning new skills would increase their engagement.[4]

Don't be afraid to make the work challenging.

Here, in fact, is the crux of it all: Make the work so challenging that it requires you to put the person who can actually *excel* at it into the role. Think about this for a moment. It's a good way to ensure you have the right person in the right role.

One of my employees just couldn't do his job. It wasn't a matter of integrity or effort. But his effort was wasted because he wasn't the right fit.

Sometimes a person is right for the job but the time frame doesn't match the project. Resist giving someone three weeks to accomplish a one-week project because you're afraid of pushback.

Expect more.

Impose tighter deadlines. Your people will actually work more efficiently and feel greater job satisfaction.

These are ways to get better performance. But you'll never know if you don't measure.

The Right Way to Measure

Someone I know in a financial group works all the time, including nights, but none of his colleagues has a clue what he's doing. He's not turning out more work because his production doesn't exceed anyone else's.

Other workers I know seem to be available 24/7. They complain-brag about the 14-hour days they put in, even posting about it (tweeting about working isn't working, by the way).

More, in these cases, definitely isn't more.

Never rely on time and presence as measures of employee productivity. The hidden cost to the "butts in seats" mindset is that we become patient and forgiving of poor quality output as long as we perceive high effort.

The point of work is to produce high-quality work. Effort might make for a great movie script about a Notre Dame walk-on, but output is what our customers are buying (or not buying). Instead, agree on the expected deliverables, the quality they should entail, and when you can expect them. Also, make sure you're not the one slowing everything down. Be the conduit, not the bottleneck.

Sometimes bosses sabotage the process, a more-than-common problem in midlevel management. For example, a lower-level employee is finishing work too quickly. Her manager, wanting to ease his own workload, tells her to slow down.

Two problems stand out: bad management and excess staff. But the boss doesn't want to lose headcount, so he clogs the workflow.

Great. Bureaucracy and bloated budget intact, complete with a bored employee who's ready to quit.

And against all apparent reason, the company retains the bad manager.

Measurement needs to occur at all levels so that everyone is accomplishing work that matters.

This book is dedicated to eliminating the distractions that prevent people from doing focused work. That also means they need *enough* work and work that challenges them. It's your job to provide it.

But There Just Isn't Enough Work

What if there's simply not enough work to do? Start by keeping a notebook of "Things that would make the team better." (I use Evernote; see Chapter 12 or more on this.) Then assign tasks as they occur to you.

Ad Hoc Projects. This is work that would improve your team or organization. It's not urgent or part of anyone's job description, but it could yield amazing dividends.

Culture Builders. Select a capable person to head a monthly lunch in which colleagues enjoy great food and learn about each other.

Training. Let people create videos or programs on a new management technique, technology that could help, or maybe even vital soft skills for today's workplace.

Research. Pick someone to examine the competition, TED Talks that would benefit the team, or efficiency tools and techniques. I like to joke that one of the best ways to improve your tech is to consult whoever wears a *Star Wars* T-shirt (though *Star Trek* and *Dr. Who* fans will also do). The person will love the assignment, and the results will save you time and money.

Each of these tasks will also showcase strengths and skills that you, and maybe even your people themselves, didn't know they had. It might even encourage them to develop new ones.

The best job descriptions are elastic, not fixed. Who knows where new sources of inspiration will carry your team?

Now That I have Your Attention . . .

For Section 7 reflection questions, summary video, and next step resources, please visit focuswise.com/book

CHAPTER 25

The Focus-Wise Leader

We are in an ocean of more than just distraction. The full force of the storm with all its winds directs its force at you. And that's just what is on the surface. Beneath, there is another force, often ignored by amateur navigators, but no less powerful—the undercurrent.

Jessica took the job at a small chemical manufacturing company because of the opportunity. The salary was lower than she could have gotten on the open market, but the owner, Tom, was 75 years old and promised to sell the company to her in time. She quickly learned the challenges the organization faced. In particular, the COO was a problem. Tom texted Jessica often, expressing his frustration with the COO on topics ranging from communication style to work ethic (even citing his weight as clear evidence of laziness).

One day, while Jessica was getting pizzas brought up to floor workers for meeting production goals the previous month, she overheard Tom tell the COO that she was being selfish and trying to purchase the company.

She learned that day what others had known for years. Tom is the kind of leader who thrives on keeping others smaller than him. Tom worked actively to keep the COO and Jessica at odds with each other. He created an enemy-of-my-enemy-is-my-friend culture. Of course, the result was dysfunction and a stagnating bottom line.

Jessica's story is an example of the undercurrent in action. The undercurrent is a force that drives how you respond to what life throws at you. It's the outcome of your experiences and beliefs. Some might call it attitude or mindset, but it goes deeper than that. Much like in an ocean, you can't see the undercurrent, but if you've ever been sucked up in one, you know it's a powerful force you must always be on guard against.

Organizations have undercurrents. So do people. They can both be dangerous. The undercurrent of your life is perhaps the most powerful because of the way it influences everything—your leadership decisions, your goals, what you pay attention to, what you ignore, what makes you laugh, what offends you, what you can't let go, what you can't remember, and so much more.

It's never been easier to ignore the undercurrent. Why would you focus on what's under the ocean when there is a massive storm in your face? We live in a world that allows us to not only consume endlessly (thus avoiding the space required for introspection) but to also consume only the information that reaffirms where our undercurrent has led us (fake news, anyone?).

The problem with ignoring the undercurrent is that, as a leader, it profoundly influences your team, your family, your friends, your spheres of influence, and your personal growth.

This is now the time to examine your undercurrent, to be honest about how you naturally respond to others. If you ignore it, you'll never get off the raft, no matter how many tools you provide yourself and your team.

There are two key areas where we will find undercurrents that effective leaders must be actively aware of: power and perspective.

Power

How much power do you feel over your past, present, and future situations? In my work with leaders across the globe, I've seen the following raft mindset approaches to power.

The Victim. It's always someone else's fault. *Who can we blame? We didn't get the deal because of Rick.* I once challenged someone on this mindset, saying, "You tend to blame others for anything in your life that doesn't work out." Their response? "Yeah, I get that from my mom." This type of leader always seeks to take credit and give blame rather than giving credit and taking blame. The victim believes they have *no power*.

The Puppet Master. I will take control over all things and all people. I use every available tool to manipulate, coerce, shame, confuse, and cajole to get what I want. The puppet master wants power over everyone. Ironically, this undercurrent is the same as the victim leader's. They assert control because they remember a time they had none and are terrified of that ever happening again.

How much power do you have to change *yourself*?

The Talented Underachiever. We are who we are. I am great at certain things. I am bad at certain things. This will not change. Carol Dweck, a professor at Stanford University, calls this the fixed mindset in her book *Mindset: The New Psychology of Success.*[1] And it's devastating for your future.

The Toddler. This leader throws tantrums, screams, and loses it often. Then he is happy again (and thinks everyone else should be too). The toddler leader believes his emotional state is something that makes him who he is. And he can't control it. So why would you be offended by it?

Perspective

Much like with power, there are common types of raft mindsets when it comes to perspective.

The Narcissist. Everything is about them. So when a colleague works late, the response is, "Always gotta make me look bad." Folks are late to a meeting because they don't respect the leader, not because they hit traffic. The narcissistic leader is incapable of imagining a world outside themselves.

The Jealous. For the jealous leader, your success is her failure. *Tom got the day off before a holiday! That should be reserved for veterans! He's only been here 14 years.* For this leader, it's always you win, I lose. *You won the big client—the one I have never spoken to and didn't know existed? How can that be?!* For the jealous leader, everything is a zero-sum game. They see the world as a pie. Anytime someone else gets a great piece, that's less for them.

The Don Quixote. This leader is always right. The other side is always wrong, stupid, evil, manipulative, nefarious, corrupt, and worthy of death. None of this, of course, is true. They're just the windmills he's constructed so he'll have something to fight.

The Aggrandizer. For this leader, nothing is ever small. *A client complained? We now have a global crisis. Did you see what Amy did? She sent the doc to the client in Times New Roman. We use Arial font! Get the whole team together to meet on this!* Everything is an excuse for an explosion. This leader believes whatever they are currently engaged in is the entire world.

The Pessimist. Best quarter ever? Doesn't matter; it's going to get worse.

The real secret? These raft mindsets are knee-jerk responses to losing one's sense of control. In every case, they are fundamentally about focusing on the wrong thing—and they are all inherently self-focused rather than people- and organization-focused.

The focus-wise leader can see the world and circumstances for what they really are and, in the process, easily steer out of dangerous undercurrents of power. They aren't afraid to ask themselves questions like, "What parts of my past am I allowing to dictate the way I view the world and the things I choose to see? Am I consistently negative? When have I walked around with negativity, suspicion, and pessimism?" To a hammer, everything is a nail. And to a nail, most things are perceived as hammers. Do you see yourself as a nail—and everything else as a hammer trying to hit you?

The focus-wise leader knows something else about undercurrents: When one is not taking us where we want to go, we can find new ones. That is the power of getting off the raft and onto the sailboat. Perhaps the core of being a focus-wise leader is being aware of the undercurrent and using every tool at your disposal to ensure it's taking you in the right direction.

What Are Better Undercurrents for Power?

Instead of feeling powerless or needing to be all powerful, we can accurately gauge where our power begins and ends. We can take control of ourselves and our response to a situation. We can also know what isn't ours to control. We can help other boats, too, without trying to commandeer them. We can give them the parts of the sail, but we can't make them sail.

For perspective, we can direct our boat toward helping others rather than being destructively self-focused—toward an abundance rather than poverty mindset. We can remind ourselves that comparison is the thief of joy (as my old choir teacher would often say) and that a rising tide raises all boats. The focus-wise leader values a diversity of views and experiences rather than being Don Quixote fighting enemies that don't exist. A better undercurrent with perspective spotlights both the importance and triviality of any particular moment and reminds us that, though our work deserves full effort, our kids will be happy to see us no matter how the client meeting turns out. The focus-wise leader is an optimist rather than a pessimist.

How Do We Shift Undercurrents?

We talked in Chapter 6 about how our past experiences shape our current perspective. The more we do something, the more we think about something, the easier and less exhaustive it is to continue to do and think about it.

I once heard we have as many as 100,000 thoughts every day (I have no idea how that can be measured). Most of them are mundane. *Cool shoes. Where's the soap? That steak smells great. Bad clothing choice.*

What we consistently see, hear, and think about—what we focus on—becomes what we believe. What we believe then dictates the way we behave.

To change our undercurrents, we need to move from passive thinking to active thinking. Here are some great ways to do so.

Manage Your Inputs

I watched way too much *Murder She Wrote*, *Unsolved Mysteries*, and *Matlock* as a kid. Add in that I grew up during the era of "stranger danger" and I came to believe every car was going to kidnap me, every knock at the door was a robber, and any crime could be solved in 30 minutes by Angela Lansbury (that is probably true; she is amazing).

My parents once came home to their fourth-grade son holding a steak knife just in case. This all changed when I stopped watching crime dramas.

It's amazing how much what we put into our brain shapes what comes out of it.

If you want to become a sail mindset leader, you need to change your inputs. Listen to growth-oriented podcasts. Limit your news updates to summaries rather than constant downloads (which is made to expose anxiety and fear to keep you watching). Intentionally read intelligent perspectives from "the other side"—and actually contend with those perspectives rather than dismissing them. Surround yourself with people who exhibit sail mindset mentalities.

When you do this, you'll find that, just like when I stopped watching crime dramas, your view of the world will radically change. And so will the effectiveness of your leadership.

Exercise the Gratitude Muscle

My daily journaling process takes fewer than 10 minutes. It starts with 10 gratitudes. It's amazing how much easier it is to see the good of life when you start every day reminding yourself of it. Optimism is an undercurrent you want to be in if you want more success (for more on this, check out Shawn Achor's book *The Happiness Advantage*). My wife and I also include three gratitudes from the day during meals together. Research shows this can noticeably change your undercurrent in a mere month.

Consider the Model

Who, honestly, is your hero? Your hero is the person you think about when you think of success. It's the person you most want to impress. This person is the model of cool. And whether we realize it or not, we will start looking more and more like them.

I spent a period of my life thinking someone was the coolest guy in the room when, in fact, his life was nothing like what I actually wanted. Brilliant? Yes. Confident? For sure. Who I wanted to become?

Not remotely. Yet, my behavior started subtly looking more and more like his. I unconsciously set him up as the marker that then shifted my own projection of my future. Actively consider who you truly admire, and actively decide whether to accept or reject that choice—or risk ending up places that wreck potential.

Get Rational about the Emotional

Hansel says he's *overwhelmed* by the exam; Gretel says she's *excited*. Hansel and Gretel have the same IQ, same GPA; they even studied together using all the same resources. Guess who does better on the exam. Here's the thing: Positive excitement and negative anxiety are, in most ways, the same biochemical reaction. Turns out the story we tell ourselves *about* that biochemical reaction has a pretty big impact on our performance. You can't control that biochemical reaction. You can control how you interpret it. And, like magic, anxiety becomes energy.

We can make choices that label and reappraise so that we can capture our emotions rather than be victims of them. Is your emotional state of being helping or hurting you?

Step 1: Label It. Literally acknowledge the emotion you are experiencing. By simply becoming aware of it, you are actually reducing its power. Like Harry Potter using Lord Voldemort's name when the other wizards lived in fear of it. The science behind this is fascinating. When you label an emotion, you activate the part of your brain used for rational processing (prefrontal and temporal regions).[2] In doing so, it reduces the power of the emotional part of your brain (amygdala), setting you up for step 2.

Step 2: Reappraise. Put the emotion in its proper context. Emotions bring focus. And typically, whatever you are focusing on at the moment is less important than you feel it is. By simply recontextualizing the experience, the arousing emotion no longer controls you. For instance, "I'm angry right now because a situation is costing me $400. These people don't really know me. It's not personal. It's a bad business practice. And it's not worth my time."

This is particularly critical for you as a leader. Your people pay attention to your emotional cues. They react, often unconsciously, to signs of anger, sadness, excitement, and joy. As the late iconic Stanford researcher Clifford Nass says, "The human brain is so exquisitely attuned to emotion, so obsessed with it, and so good at detecting it, that even the slightest markers of emotion can have an enormous impact on how the brain behaves."[3]

Ultimately, Know Thyself

As Edwin Friedman writes (fittingly, using a sailing analogy):

> Every experienced boater knows that when one is docking or pulling away from the dock, all efforts to try to overcome wind and current by simply trying harder generally do not work. Mother Nature wins most contests of will unless one has very great amounts of power at hand. Experienced sailors have learned that far better than fighting those natural forces is to position oneself so that they will, in their own natural way, aid rather than frustrate one's intent. How, then, does one go with the flow and still take the lead? Answer: by positioning oneself in such a way that the natural forces of emotional life carry one in the right direction. The key to that positioning is the leader's own self-differentiation, by which I mean his or her own capacity to be a nonanxious presence, a challenging presence, a well-defined presence, and a paradoxical presence. Differentiation is not about being coercive, manipulative, reactive, pursuing or invasive, but being *rooted* in the leader's own sense of self rather than focused on that of his or her followers.[4]

The ocean of today is not easy to navigate. It's filled with distractions, temptations, and assaults on our worth—a perfect storm. Being the captain at sea is not for the faint of heart. It's far easier to sit on a raft and let the ocean take the lead.

But you have the right vessel, the right equipment, the wind, and the right undercurrents. You know the conditions, and you are not alone. Join us as we journey together in this exciting, chaotic, distracting, noisy, wavy, stormy, constantly connected workplace. And amid all of life's distractions, sail on.

ABOUT THE AUTHORS

Curt Steinhorst

Curt Steinhorst is on a mission to rescue us from our distracted selves. Having spent years studying the impact of tech on human behavior, Curt founded Focuswise, a consultancy that equips organizations to overcome the distinct challenges of the constantly connected workplace. He is also a certified speaker at the Center for Generational Kinetics, the premier organization for generational research in North America.

Diagnosed with ADD as a child, Curt knows intimately the challenges companies face in keeping the attention of today's distracted workforce and customer. He has coached executives, TV personalities, and well-known professional athletes on how to effectively communicate and create focus when they speak to audiences, lead their employees, and engage their customers.

Curt's unique insight and entertaining speaking style has captured the attention of audiences worldwide. He speaks more than seventy-five times a year to everyone from leadership associations and global nonprofits to Fortune 100 companies.

Curt is a proud graduate of Texas A&M University, where he served a term as president of his class. Curt lives in Frisco, Texas, with his wife, Kimi, and two sons, Rand and Reed.

Jonathan McKee

Jonathan McKee is the author of over 20 books including *52 Ways to Connect with Your Smartphone Obsessed Kid*, *The New Breed*. and *The Teens Guide to Social Media and Mobile Devices*. Jonathan is an expert on youth culture, speaking to parents and leaders worldwide about raising this next generation of leaders. He has over 20 years working with teenagers and founded a nonprofit organization, TheSource4Parents .com providing free resources and training to anyone working with young people. Jonathan, his wife Lori, and their three kids live in California.

Acknowledgments

Where It Begins and Ends

To my wife: Every word spoken in front of an audience and written in a chapter comes at a cost. It's another moment that my wife, Kimi, doesn't get on the couch talking over wine, walking the dogs, breaking bread at the dinner table, or simply cuddling in bed with the man who promised her all those things when we committed to do life together. It's another minute of caring for two wonderfully loving, woefully dependent, equal parts fragile and strong-willed, foolishly risky, prone to self-harm, 100 percent boy, and laughter-instigating children without her partner to sub in, provide a second pair of eyes, kiss-fix the ouchy, correct the bad behavior, or tuck the "not tired" kid into bed. And yet she continues to encourage and support this dream, fully aware of the cost. I knew it was a good decision in 2012, but she has far exceeded my expectation of what good could be.

To my parents and sister: If I told you what my childhood was like, you would think I lived in a fantasy land. I am the product of parents who love each other, who pushed their kids to excellence but didn't demand unrealistic perfection, who celebrated our successes but didn't need it to compensate for their own shortcomings, who disciplined but didn't raise their voices, who let us be kids but wouldn't let us stay kids. The adult version of that child risks and relates radically differently because of such a rare and firm foundation. Not to say it was all perfect. It's not fair being the younger brother of the perfect sister. (A single B would have been nice, as would the occasional getting caught in a lie.) But then I wouldn't have the sounding board I cherish or encouragement I respect if my older sister wasn't so damn smart, hard-working, disciplined, or kind.

To Pap: I bear the name of my grandfather, Curtis Wheat. He whistled everywhere he went. People don't whistle anymore. It's impossible to be around someone who whistles without having the joy rub off on you. He married his middle school sweetheart, my Mammaw. Her strength made our family a single unit. I wear their wedding band. The standard has been set. I miss him.

Along the Way

To the Marketplace One community: My life can be effectively divided between PM1 (Pre-Marketplace One community) and AM1 (in the age of Marketplace One community). For late nights, whiskey tastings, honest questions, serious disagreements, big hugs, guttural laughter, real tears, and the feeling of *oikos* whenever I'm among you. Specifically, Lukas Naugle for being the first to tell me my business was unfocused and my message was distraction and for continuing to let me lean on him for strategy and wisdom.

To the Focuswise core team (Jared, Steve, Knic): For keeping me focused, making me look good, and always having my back.

To the Center for Generational Kinetics: For their insight, support, mentorship, partnership, commitment to excellence, and letting me come along for the ride.

The Words on the Page

Growing up, I wrote my debate cases while en route to the speech tournament. I should not have a book that bears my name. And of course, I wouldn't if not for the village of people who played an integral role in every stage of its development.

To Paul Matthies: The greatest teammate, partner, advocate, encourager, business operator, and gift giver in the world. I wonder if most attempts by easily distracted visionaries fail simply because they haven't found Paul. And no, he's not available.

To Jake Johnson and Vic Vogler: Any help this book offers, any success this project experiences, any ideas that make sense on these pages will be because of your writing prowess.

To Trevor Boehm: For bringing order and a plan to the chaos I created for this book project.

To Greg Johnson: For taking a risk on me years before the growth and sticking with me through years of running in circles on this book project.

To Josh Farrar and Michael Thate, PhD: Whose ideas and words are littered throughout the pages of this book.

To Mick Lesko and Daniel Turner: Their care for this project because of their care for me would be rare at any time in history. In a world that limits friendship to the convenient, their approach serves as a reminder of the limitless life-giving nature of that true and rare gift of friendship.

As Zig Ziglar would say (relayed through Bryan Flanagan, another mentor who deserves more than this single line), "Of all the attitudes we can acquire, surely the attitude of gratitude is the most important and by far the most life-changing." It's not difficult to carry this attitude with the people who surround me and this project. Thank you.

NOTES

PROLOGUE

1. Lulu Chang, "Americans Spend an Alarming Amount of Time Checking Social Media on Their Phones," Digital Trends, updated June 13, 2015, http://www.digitaltrends.com/mobile/informate-report-social-media-smartphone-use/.
2. "Growth of Time Spent on Mobile Devices Slows," eMarketer, October 7, 2015, https://www.emarketer.com/Article/Growth-of-Time-Spent-on-Mobile-Devices-Slows/1013072.
3. Alex Cocotas, "88% of U.S. Consumers Use Mobile as Second Screen While Watching TV," Business Insider, May 20, 2013, http://www.businessinsider.com/a-majority-uses-mobile-as-second-screen-2013-5.

SECTION 1
CHAPTER 1

1. "The Shape of Email," Mimecast, October 2012, http://www.tbline.nl/index_htm_files/Mimecast-WP-Shape-of-Email-Report-Consumer.pdf.
2. Brigid Schulte, "Work Interruptions Can Cost You 6 Hours a Day. An Efficiency Expert Explains How to Avoid Them," *The Washington Post*, June 1, 2015, https://www.washingtonpost.com/news/inspired-life/wp/2015/06/01/interruptions-at-work-can-cost-you-up-to-6-hours-a-day-heres-how-to-avoid-them/?utm_term=.a12d4f6d9e9e.
3. Schulte, "Work Interruptions."
4. Bryan College, "How Are Multitasking Millennials Impacting Today's Workplace?" accessed April 28, 2017, http://www.bryan.edu/news/multitasking-at-work.
5. Kris Duggan, "Feeling Distracted by Politics? 29% of Employees Are Less Productive after U.S. Election," BetterWorks, February 7, 2017, https://blog.betterworks.com/feeling-distracted-politics-29-employees-less-productive-u-s-election/.
6. Juline E. Mills, Bo Hu, Srikanth Beldona, and Joan Clay, "Cyber-slacking! A Wired-Workplace Liability Issue," *The Cornell Hotel and*

Restaurant Administration Quarterly, 42, no. 5 (2001): 34–47, http://www
.sciencedirect.com/science/article/pii/S0010880401800562.

7. "The Engaged Workplace," Gallup, accessed May 1, 2017, http://www
.gallup.com/services/190118/engaged-workplace.aspx.

Chapter 2

1. Thomas H. Davenport and John C. Beck, *The Attention Economy: Understanding the New Currency of Business* (Boston: Harvard Business School, 2001), 3.
2. Nora D. Volkow, "Drugs, Brains, and Behavior: The Science of Addiction," National Institute on Drug Abuse, July 2014, https://www
.drugabuse.gov/publications/drugs-brains-behavior-science-addiction.
3. Volkow, "Drugs, Brains, and Behavior."

Chapter 3

1. Sean Casey, "2016 Nielsen Social Media Report," Nielsen, January 17, 2017, 6, http://www.nielsen.com/content/dam/corporate/us/en/reports-downloads/2017-reports/2016-nielsen-social-media-report.pdf.
2. Jane Helpern, "Why Generation Z Are Deleting Their Social Media Accounts and Going Offline," *Vice*, October 12, 2015, https://i-d.vice
.com/en_gb/article/why-generation-z-are-deleting-their-social-media-accounts-and-going-offline.
3. Casey, "Nielsen Report," 6.
4. Joshua S. Rubinstein et al., "Executive Control of Cognitive Processes in Task Switching," *Journal of Experimental Psychology: Human Perception and Performance*, 27, no. 4 (2001): 763–797, http://umich.edu/~bcalab/documents/RubinsteinMeyerEvans2001.pdf.
5. David Rock, *Your Brain at Work: Strategies for Overcoming Distraction, Regaining Focus, and Working Smarter All Day Long* (New York: HarperCollins Publishers, 2009), 36.
6. The Engaged Workplace," Gallup, accessed May 1, 2017, http://www
.gallup.com/services/190118/engaged-workplace.aspx.

Section 2
Chapter 4

1. Timothy J. Buschman et al., "Top-Down Versus Bottom-Up Control of Attention in the Prefrontal and Posterior Parietal Cortices,"

Science, 315, no. 5820 (2007): 1860–1862, http://ekmillerlab.mit.edu/wp-content/uploads/2013/03/Buschman-and-Miller-Science-2007.pdf. Yair Pinto et al., "Bottom-Up and Top-Down Attention Are Independent," *Journal of Vision*, 13, no. 3 (2013): 16, http://jov.arvojournals.org/article.aspx?articleid=2194099 or http://dx.doi.org/10.1167/13.3.16.

2. Eli Saslow, "Freak of Nurture," ESPN, July 13, 2012, http://www.espn.com/tennis/story/_/id/8132800/has-novak-djokovic-become-fittest-athlete-ever-espn-magazine.

3. Joshua S. Rubinstein et al., "Executive Control of Cognitive Processes in Task Switching," *Journal of Experimental Psychology: Human Perception and Performance*, 27, no. 4 (2001): 763–797, http://umich.edu/~bcalab/documents/RubinsteinMeyerEvans2001.pdf.

4. Jason M. Watson and David L. Strayer, "Supertaskers: Profiles in Extraordinary Multitasking Ability," *Psychonomic Bulletin & Review*, 17, no. 4 (2010): 479–485, https://www.ncbi.nlm.nih.gov/pubmed/20702865.

5. "Emails 'Hurt More than Pot,'" CNN.com, April 22, 2005, http://www.cnn.com/2005/WORLD/europe/04/22/text.iq/.

6. Rubinstein et al., "Cognitive Processes in Task Switching."

7. Steven Sweldens, "In Defense of Multitasking," INSEAD, February 21, 2017, http://knowledge.insead.edu/career/in-defence-of-multitasking-5281.

8. Mirjam Tuk et al., "Inhibitory Spillover: Increased Urination Urgency Facilitates Impulse Control in Unrelated Domains," SSRN, December 10, 2010, https://ssrn.com/abstract=1720956 or http://dx.doi.org/10.2139/ssrn.1720956.

9. Tuk et al., "Inhibitory Spillover."

10. Sweldens, "In Defense of Multitasking."

11. Ravi Mehta et al., "Is Noise Always Bad? Exploring the Effects of Ambient Noise on Creative Cognition," *Journal of Consumer Research*, 39, no. 4 (2012): 784–799, http://www.jstor.org/stable/10.1086/665048.

12. Jill Pease, "UF Study Shows Benefits of Multi-Tasking on Exercise," University of Florida, June 2, 2015, http://news.ufl.edu/archive/2015/06/uf-study-shows-benefits-of-multi-tasking-on-exercise.html.

CHAPTER 5

1. Walter Mischel, Ebbe B. Ebbesen, and Antonette Raskoff Zeiss, "Cognitive and Attentional Mechanisms in Delay of Gratification," *Journal of Personality and Social Psychology*, 21, no. 2 (1972), 204–218, http://psycnet.apa.org/journals/psp/21/2/204/.

Chapter 6

1. Steven Sweldens, "In Defense of Multitasking," INSEAD, February 21, 2017, http://knowledge.insead.edu/career/in-defence-of-multitasking-5281.
2. Robin Nixon, "Brain Food: How to Eat Smart," LIVESCIENCE, January 7, 2009, http://www.livescience.com/3186-brain-food-eat-smart.html.
3. Nixon, "Brain Food."
4. Shai Danziger et al., "Extraneous Factors in Judicial Decisions," Proceedings of the National Academy of Sciences of the United States of America, 108, no. 17 (2011): 6889–6892, http://www.pnas.org/content/108/17/6889.abstract.
5. Marco Hafner et al., "Why Sleep Matters—the Economic Costs of Insufficient Sleep," Rand Corporation, 2016, http://www.rand.org/pubs/research_reports/RR1791.html.
6. Cecilia Kang, "Google Crunches Data on Munching in Office," *The Washington Post*, September 1, 2013, https://www.washingtonpost.com/business/technology/google-crunches-data-on-munching-in-office/2013/09/01/3902b444-0e83-11e3-85b6-d27422650fd5_story.html?utm_term=.218047a6880e.
7. Maria Popova, "Debunking the Myth of the 10,000-Hours Rule: What It Actually Takes to Reach Genius-Level Excellence," Brain Pickings, accessed June 1, 2017, https://www.brainpickings.org/2014/01/22/daniel-goleman-focus-10000-hours-myth/.

Section 3
Chapter 7

1. Rachel Feltman, "Most Men Would Rather Shock Themselves than Be Alone with Their Thoughts," *The Washington Post*, July 3, 2014, https://www.washingtonpost.com/news/to-your-health/wp/2014/07/03/most-men-would-rather-shock-themselves-than-be-alone-with-their-thoughts/?utm_term=.746beb1e189a.
2. Feltman, "Most Men Would Rather Shock Themselves."
3. Justin Talbot-Zorn and Leigh Marz, "The Busier You Are, the More You Need Quiet Time," *Harvard Business Review*, March 17, 2017, https://hbr.org/2017/03/the-busier-you-are-the-more-you-need-quiet-time.
4. Jennifer Porter, "Why You Should Make Time for Self-Reflection (Even If You Hate Doing It)," *Harvard Business Review*, March 21, 2017, https://hbr.org/2017/03/why-you-should-make-time-for-self-reflection-even-if-you-hate-doing-it.

CHAPTER 8

1. Janet Pogue McLaurin, "Gensler's 2013 Workplace Survey: Balance in Any Environment," July 22, 2013, http://www.gensleron.com/work/2013/7/22/genslers-2013-workplace-survey-balance-in-any-environment.html.

2. Brie Weiler Reynolds, "Survey: Only 7% of Workers Say They're Most Productive in the Office," FlexJobs, August 26, 2016, https://www.flexjobs.com/blog/post/survey-workers-most-productive-in-the-office/.

3. George Musser, "The Origin of Cubicles and the Open-Plan Office," *Scientific American*, August 17, 2009, https://www.scientificamerican.com/article/the-origin-of-cubicles-an/.

4. Rachel Gillet, "Mark Zuckerberg Shows That He Works at the Same Kind of Desk as Everyone Else," *Business Insider*, September 15, 2015, http://www.businessinsider.com/mark-zuckerberg-virtual-tour-frank-gehry-designed-building-2015-9.

5. Lindsey Kaufman, "Google Got It Wrong. The Open-Office Trend Is Destroying the Workplace," *The Washington Post*, December 30, 2014, https://www.washingtonpost.com/posteverything/wp/2014/12/30/google-got-it-wrong-the-open-office-trend-is-destroying-the-workplace/?utm_term=.c5e368ff9397.

6. Genevieve Douglas, "Office Space Design May Affect Worker Productivity," Bloomberg BNA, March 3, 2017, https://www.bna.com/office-space-design-n57982084770/.

7. Gillet, "Mark Zuckerberg."

8. Sarah Green Carmichael, "Research: Cubicles Are the Absolute Worst," *Harvard Business Review*, November 13, 2013, https://hbr.org/2013/11/research-cubicles-are-the-absolute-worst.

9. J. Maureen Henderson, "Why the Open-Concept Office Trend Needs to Die," *Forbes*, December 16, 2014, https://www.forbes.com/sites/jmaureenhenderson/2014/12/16/why-the-open-concept-office-trend-needs-to-die/#7eeeab03603a.

10. Maria Konnikova, "The Open-Office Trap," *The New Yorker*, January 7, 2014, http://www.newyorker.com/business/currency/the-open-office-trap.

11. Musser, "The Origin of Cubicles and the Open-Plan Office."

12. "Depreciation of Business Assets," Intuit TurboTax, accessed May 18, 2017, https://turbotax.intuit.com/tax-tools/tax-tips/Small-Business-Taxes/Depreciation-of-Business-Assets/INF12091.html?PID=7099101&SID=35871X943606X640c5d4caf670c4d1fd6ac4b02ed6e17&CID=all_cjtto-7099101_int&ref_id=534b7dbb343711e781461803730e3c59_130201446664459306:M5PqnhjqA2Xq.

13. Jeff Pochepan, "Bad Mood in the Workplace? Try Changing the Lights," *Inc.*, March 23, 2017, https://www.inc.com/jeff-pochepan/these-office-lighting-changes-will-improve-your-mood-and-productivity.html.

14. Reynolds, "Survey: Only 7% of Workers Say They're Most Productive in the Office."

15. Sue Shellenbarger, "Why You Can't Concentrate at Work," *The Wall Street Journal*, May 9, 2017, https://www.wsj.com/articles/why-you-cant-concentrate-at-work-1494342840.

16. McLaurin, "Gensler's 2013 Workplace Survey."

Chapter 9

1. Gloria Mark et al., "'A Pace Not Dictated by Electrons': An Empirical Study of Work without Email," Proceedings of the SIGCHI Conference on Human Factors in Computing Systems (Austin: ACM, 2012), 555–564, http://dl.acm.org/citation.cfm?id=2207754.

Section 4
Chapter 10

1. "2016 Workplace Index," Staples Business Advantage, accessed May 11, 2017, https://www.staplesadvantage.com/sites/workplace-index/index.html.

2. Heather R. Huhman, "How to Deal with These 4 Employee Frustrations," *Entrepreneur*, August 15, 2016, https://www.entrepreneur.com/article/280543.

3. "The Digital Workplace Initiative," Konica Minolta, 2017, 1, https://www.konicaminolta.co.uk/fileadmin/content/uk/Business_Solutions/PDF/digital-workplace-initiative.pdf.

4. Martin Heidegger, edit. and trans. by Julian Young and Kenneth Haynes, *Off the Beaten Track* (Cambridge: Cambridge University Press, 2002), 54.

5. Adam Alter, "How Technology Gets Us Hooked," *The Guardian*, February 28, 2017, https://www.theguardian.com/technology/2017/feb/28/how-technology-gets-us-hooked.

6. B. F. Skinner, "A case history in scientific method," *American Psychologist*, Vol 11(5), May 1956), 221–233.

7. Ofir Turel et al., "Examination of Neural Systems Sub-Serving Facebook 'Addiction,'" *Psychological Reports*, 115, no. 3 (2014): 675–695, https://www.ncbi.nlm.nih.gov/pubmed/25489985.

8. Rebecca Strong, "Brain Scans Show How Facebook and Cocaine Addictions Are the Same," BostInno, February 2, 2015, http://bostinno .streetwise.co/2015/02/03/why-delete-facebook-facebook-addiction-similar-to-cocaine-addiction/.

9. Anderson Cooper, "What Is 'Brain Hacking'? Tech Insiders on Why You Should Care," *CBS News*, April 9, 2017, http://www.cbsnews.com/news/ brain-hacking-tech-insiders-60-minutes/.

CHAPTER 11

1. Dennis McCafferty, "What to Look for in Collaborative Tools," CIO Insight, accessed July 17, 2017, http://www.cioinsight.com/it-strategy/ messaging-collaboration/slideshows/what-to-look-for-in-collaborative tools.html.

2. McCafferty, "Collaborative Tools."

CHAPTER 12

1. Vincent Del Giudice and Wei Lu, "America's Rich Get Richer and the Poor Get Replaced by Robots," Bloomberg, April 26, 2017, https:// www.bloomberg.com/news/articles/2017-04-26/america-s-rich-poor-divide-keeps-ballooning-as-robots-take-jobs.

CHAPTER 13

1. Katie Johnston, "Firms Step up Employee Monitoring at Work," *The Boston Globe*, February 19, 2016, https://www.bostonglobe.com/ business/2016/02/18/firms-step-monitoring-employee-activities-work/ 2l5hoCjsEZWA0bp10BzPrN/story.html.

2. Theodore Kinni, "Monitoring Your Employee's Every Emotion," *MIT Sloan Management Review*, September 15, 2016, http://sloanreview.mit .edu/article/tech-savvy-monitoring-your-employees-every-emotion/.

3. Lee Michael Katz, "Monitoring Employee Productivity: Proceed with Caution," Society for Human Resource Management, June 1, 2015, https://www.shrm.org/hr-today/news/hr-magazine/pages/0615-employee-monitoring.aspx.

4. Will Knight, "Socially Sensitive AI Software Coaches Call-Center Workers," *MIT Technology Review*, January 31, 2017, https://www .technologyreview.com/s/603529/socially-sensitive-ai-software-coaches-call-center-workers/.

5. Jon Hyman, "Workplace Social Media Policies Must Account for Generational Issues," *Business Management Daily: The Legal Workplace Blog*, January 24, 2013, http://www.businessmanagementdaily.com/34411/workplace-social-media-policies-must-account-for-generational-issues.

6. Don Troop, "Harrisburg U.'s Social Media Blackout Is More of a Brownout," *The Chronicle of Higher Education*, September 16, 2010, http://www.chronicle.com/article/Harrisburg-Us-Social-Media/124510/.

7. Kevan Lee, "The Advantages and Workflows of Fully Transparent Email," Buffer, June 16, 2014, https://open.buffer.com/buffer-transparent-email/.

8. James Brooks, "Cyborgs at Work: Employees Getting Implanted with Microchips," *AP News*, April 3, 2017, https://apnews.com/4fdcd5970f4f4871961b69eeff5a6585/cyborgs-work-employees-getting-implanted-microchips.

SECTION 5
CHAPTER 14

1. "Email Statistics Report, 2017–2019," The Radicati Group, Inc., 2017, http://www.radicati.com/wp/wp-content/uploads/2017/01/Email-Statistics-Report-2017-2021-Executive-Summary.pdf.

2. Heinz Tschabitscher, "How Many Emails Are Sent Every Day and Other Fascinating Email Statistics," Lifewire, updated March 29, 2017, https://www.lifewire.com/how-many-emails-are-sent-every-day-1171210.

3. Craig Smith, "By the Numbers: 80+ Incredible Email Statistics and Facts (February 2017)," DMR, February 14, 2017, http://expandedramblings.com/index.php/email-statistics/.

4. Alina Tugend, "Too Many Choices: A Problem That Can Paralyze," *The New York Times*, February 26, 2017, http://www.nytimes.com/2010/02/27/your-money/27shortcuts.html.

5. Oliver Burkerman, "Meeting: Even More of a Soul-Sucking Waste of Time than You Thought," *The Guardian*, May 1, 2014, https://www.theguardian.com/news/oliver-burkeman-s-blog/2014/may/01/meetings-soul-sucking-waste-time-you-thought.

6. "Solving for the Dark Side of Metcalfe's Law," Bain Digital Brief, accessed May 18, 2017, http://www.bain.com/Images/BAIN_BRIEF_Solving_for_the_dark_side_of_Metcalfes_Law.pdf.

7. Caity Weaver, "There Is Nothing Better in the World than Talking about Yourself," Gawker, May 18, 2012, http://gawker.com/5908736/there-is-actually-nothing-better-in-the-world-than-talking-about-yourself.

CHAPTER 15

1. Kabir Sehgal, "How to Write Email with Military Precision," *Harvard Business Review*, November 22, 2016, https://hbr.org/2016/11/how-to-write-email-with-military-precision.
2. James Altucher, "33 Unusual Tips to Being a Better Writer," James Altucher, accessed May 24, 2017, http://www.jamesaltucher.com/2011/03/33-unusual-tips-become-better-writer/
3. "Emojis Use Can Give Insight into Human Behaviour: New Research," *Global Times*, January 18, 2017, http://www.globaltimes.cn/content/1029410.shtml.
4. Justin Kruger, Nicholas Epley, Jason Parker, Zhi-Wen Ng, "Egocentrism over e-mail: Can we communicate as well as we think?" *Journal of Personality and Social Psychology*, Vol 89(6), Dec 2005, 925–936. http://dx.doi.org/10.1037/0022-3514.89.6.925.

CHAPTER 16

1. Jessica Olien, "Loneliness Is Deadly," *Slate*, August 23, 2013, http://www.slate.com/articles/health_and_science/medical_examiner/2013/08/dangers_of_loneliness_social_isolation_is_deadlier_than_obesity.html.
2. Honor Whiteman, "Loneliness Alters the Immune System to Cause Illness, Study Finds," *Medical News Today*, November 24, 2015, http://www.medicalnewstoday.com/articles/303084.php.
3. David Brooks, *The Social Animal: The Hidden Sources of Love, Character, and Achievement* (New York: Random House, 2012), xvi.
4. Vittorio Gallese and Alvin Goldman, "Mirror Neurons and the Simulation Theory of Mind-Reading," *Trends in Cognitive Sciences*, 12, no. 2 (1998): 493–501, http://www.cell.com/trends/cognitive-sciences/fulltext/S1364-6613(98)01262-5?_returnURL=http%3A%2F%2Flinkinghub.elsevier.com%2Fretrieve%2Fpii%2FS1364661398012625%3Fshowall%3Dtrue.
5. Edwin H. Friedman, *A Failure of Nerve: Leadership in the Age of the Quick Fix* (New York: Church Publishing, 2007), 13–14.

SECTION 6
CHAPTER 17

1. Gianpiero Petriglieri, "Is Overwork Killing You?" *Harvard Business Review*, August 31, 2015, https://hbr.org/2015/08/is-overwork-killing-you.
2. Edward Cone and Adrianna Gregory, "When the Walls Come Down," Oxford Economics, accessed May 19, 2017, https://www.oxfordeconomics.com/when-the-walls-come-down.
3. Mark Hanrahan, "France 'Right to Disconnect' Law: Do We Need Rules to Reclaim Personal Time?" *NBC News*, January 9, 2017, http://www.nbcnews.com/news/world/france-right-disconnect-law-do-we-need-rules-reclaim-personal-n704366.
4. "After-hours email expectations negatively impact employee well-being," Phys.org, July 27, 2016, https://phys.org/news/2016-07-after-hours-email-negatively-impact-employee.html.
5. Michelle Klampe, "Maintaining an Active Sex Life May Lead to Improved Job Satisfaction, Engagement in Work," Oregon State University News and Research Communications, March 6, 2017, http://oregonstate.edu/ua/ncs/archives/2017/mar/maintaining-active-sex-life-may-lead-improved-job-satisfaction-engagement-work.

CHAPTER 18

1. Amelia Edelman, "Surprise: Millennials Are SERIOUSLY Stressed, Says Science," Refinery 29, February 6, 2017, http://www.refinery29.com/2017/02/139598/millennials-work-stress.

CHAPTER 19

1. Nick van Dam and Els van der Helm, "There's a Proven Link between Effective Leadership and Getting Enough Sleep," *Harvard Business Review*, February 16, 2016, https://hbr.org/2016/02/theres-a-proven-link-between-effective-leadership-and-getting-enough-sleep.
2. Sheena Iyengar, "How to Make Choosing Easier," TEDSalon, November 2011, https://www.ted.com/talks/sheena_iyengar_choosing_what_to_choose?language=en.
3. Stephanie Vozza, "Why Employees at Apple and Google Are More Productive," *Fast Company*, March 13, 2017, https://www.fastcompany.com/3068771/how-employees-at-apple-and-google-are-more-productive.

4. Gary Hamel and Michele Zanini, "Excess Management Is Costing the U.S. $3 Trillion per Year," *Harvard Business Review*, September 5, 2016, https://hbr.org/2016/09/excess-management-is-costing-the-us-3-trillion-per-year.

5. Carmen Nobel, "Why Productivity Suffers When Employees Are Allowed to Schedule Their Own Tasks," Working Knowledge, Harvard Business School, April 12, 2017, http://hbswk.hbs.edu/item/why-productivity-suffers-when-employees-are-allowed-to-schedule-their-own-tasks.

6. John Pencavel, "The Productivity of Working Hours," Stanford University and IZA DP, no. 8129 (2014), http://ftp.iza.org/dp8129.pdf.

7. Leo Wildrich, "The Origin of the 8-Hour Work Day and Why We Should Rethink It," Buffer Social, June 11, 2013, https://blog.bufferapp.com/optimal-work-time-how-long-should-we-work-every-day-the-science-of-mental-strength.

8. Gwen Moran, "Surprisingly Simple Ways You Can Trick Your Brain into Focusing," *Fast Company*, June 9, 2016, https://www.fastcompany.com/3060709/how-to-train-your-brain-to-focus-remember-and-have-more-breakthrou.

9. Heather Ohly, Mathew P. White, Benedict W. Wheeler, Alison Bethel, Obioha C. Ukoumunne, Vasilis Nikolaou, and Ruth Garside, "Attention Restoration Theory: A Systematic Review of the Attention Restoration Potential of Exposure to Natural Environments," *Journal of Toxicological and Environmental Health*, Part B, 19, no. 7 (2016): 305–343, http://www.tandfonline.com/doi/full/10.1080/10937404.2016.1196155.

SECTION 7
CHAPTER 20

1. Ryan Holiday, "What Are You Working Towards? Because You Better Know," Thought Catalogue, accessed July 6, 2017, http://thoughtcatalog.com/ryan-holiday/2015/09/what-are-you-working-towards-because-you-better-know/

2. Steven Weinberg, *To Explain the World: The Discovery of Modern Science* (New York: HarperCollins, 2015), 33–34.

3. Weinberg, *To Explain the World*, 33–34.

4. Christopher Chabris and Daniel Simons, "The Invisible Gorilla," 2010, http://theinvisiblegorilla.com/gorilla_experiment.html.

Chapter 21

1. Dean Anderson and Linda Ackerman Anderson, "How Command and Control as a Change Leadership Style Causes Transformational Change Efforts to Fail," Change Leader's Network, accessed May 24, 2017, http://changeleadersnetwork.com/free-resources/how-command-and-control-as-a-change-leadership-style-causes-transformational-change-efforts-to-fail.
2. Anderson and Ackerman Anderson, "Command and Control."

Chapter 22

1. John K. Mullen, "Digital Natives Are Slow to Pick up Nonverbal Cues," *Harvard Business Review*, March 16, 2012, https://hbr.org/2012/03/digital-natives-are-slow-to-pi?awid=6625338759468407697-3271.
2. Kate Davidson, "The 'Soft Skills' Employers Are Looking for," *The Wall Street Journal*, August 30, 2016, https://blogs.wsj.com/economics/2016/08/30/the-soft-skills-employers-are-looking-for/.
3. Eliana Esther Gallardo-Echenique, Luis Marqués-Molías, Mark Bullen and Jan-Willem Strijbos, "Let's Talk about Digital Learners in the Digital Era," IRRODL, June 2015, http://www.irrodl.org/index.php/irrodl/article/view/2196/3337.
4. Chris Cillizza, "Americans Read Headlines and Not Much Else," *The Washington Post*, March 19, 2014, https://www.washingtonpost.com/news/the-fix/wp/2014/03/19/americans-read-headlines-and-not-much-else/?utm_term=.24af96bd35e9.

Chapter 23

1. Stephanie Vozza, "Why Employees at Apple and Google Are More Productive," *Fast Company*, March 13, 2017, https://www.fastcompany.com/3068771/how-employees-at-apple-and-google-are-more-productive.
2. Paul Scott Anderson, "James Webb Space Telescope Arrives at Johnson Space Center for Cryogenic Testing," *America Space*, accessed May 24, 2017, http://www.americaspace.com/2017/05/16/james-webb-space-telescope-arrives-at-johnson-space-center-for-cryogenic-testing/.
3. "2017 Edelman Trust Barometer Reveals Implosion of Trust," Edelman, January 15, 2017, http://www.edelman.com/news/2017-edelman-trust-barometer-reveals-global-implosion/.
4. Marguerite Ward, "Top CEO Coach and Former Google Exec Says This Is the No. 1 Trait Great Bosses Share," CNBC, March 21, 2017,

http://www.cnbc.com/2017/03/21/former-google-exec-shares-the-no-1-trait-great-bosses-share.html.

5. Simon Sinek, "How Great Leaders Inspire Action," TEDxPuget Sound, September 2009, https://www.ted.com/talks/simon_sinek_how_great_leaders_inspire_action?language=en.

CHAPTER 24

1. Reuben Yonatan, "Survey: Almost Half of the U.S. Workforce Is Bored at Their Jobs," GETVOIP, November 9, 2015, https://getvoip.com/blog/2015/11/09/survey-americans-are-bored-at-their-jobs/.

2. Mihaly Csikszentmihalyi, *Flow: The Psychology of Optimal Experience* (New York: Harper and Row, 1990), 3.

3. "Lost Minutes: Employee Time-Wasting Examined," Paychex Worx, August 8, 2017, https://www.paychex.com/articles/human-resources/lost-minutes-employee-time-wasting-examined.

4. Emily Wiechers, "2016 Udemy Workplace Boredom Study," Udemy News, October 26, 2016, https://about.udemy.com/udemy-for-business/workplace-boredom-study/.

CHAPTER 25

1. Carol Dweck, *Mindset: The New Psychology of Success* (New York: Random House, 2006).

2. Kristen Lindquist, "Does Labeling Your Feelings Help Regulate Them?," *Emotion News*, September 9, 2016, http://emotionnews.org/does-labeling-your-feelings-help-regulate-them/.

3. Maggie Jackson, *Distracted: The Erosion of Attention and the Coming Dark Age* (New York: Prometheus Books, 2008), 192.

4. Edwin H. Friedman, *A Failure of Nerve: Leadership in the Age of the Quick Fix* (New York: Church Publishing, 2007), 229–230.

INDEX

Page references followed by *fig* indicate an illustrated figure.